GENDER,
CULTURE,
AND
PHYSICALITY

GENDER, CULTURE,

AND

PHYSICALITY

PARADOXES AND TABOOS

HELEN STERK
AND
ANNELIES KNOPPERS

LEXINGTON BOOKS
A division of
ROWMAN & LITTLEFIELD PUBLISHERS, INC.
Lanham • Boulder • New York • Toronto • Plymouth, UK

Published by Lexington Books
A division of Rowman & Littlefield Publishers, Inc.
A wholly owned subsidary of The Rowman & Littlefield Publishing Group, Inc.
4501 Forbes Boulevard, Suite 200, Lanham, Maryland 20706
http://www.lexingtonbooks.com

Estover Road, Plymouth PL6 7PY, United Kingdom

British Library Cataloguing in Publication Information Available

Library of Congress Cataloging-in-Publication Data
Sterk, Helen M., 1952-
Gender, culture, and physicality : paradoxes and taboos / Helen Sterk and
Annelies Knoppers.
    p. cm.
Includes bibliographical references and index.
ISBN 978-0-7391-3406-1 (cloth : alk. paper) — ISBN 978-0-7391-3408-5
(electronic)
1. Sex role. 2. Women—Identity. 3. Men—Identity. 4. Sex differences—Social
aspects. I. Knoppers, Annelies. II. Title.
HQ1075.S735 2010
305.3—dc22   2009038496

♾™ The paper used in this publication meets the minimum requirements of
American National Standard for Information Sciences—Permanence of Paper
for Printed Library Materials, ANSI/NISO Z39.48-1992.

Printed in the United States of America

To our mothers, who were strong role models.

To mothers and fathers, who teach
their children about social justice.

To daughters and sons, whose job
it is to degender their world.

CONTENTS

PREFACE

Is this really a postfeminist era?

Some think it is; it appears that men and women share a level playing field in life. It looks as if there is no place left where the old saws of sexism hold true and where prejudice against women routinely can be indulged. Women, not men, the argument runs, now shape the meanings of gendered practices. Discrimination has disappeared no matter what part of life is concerned, whether that is health care, interpersonal relationships, recreation, or work.

After all, the reasoning goes, women now define and dictate their own treatment in the quintessentially female act of giving birth, right?

Not really. Around the world, birthing practices tend more and more toward a masculine model of control over women rather than a model that engages women as partners. For example, in America, even though birthing practices and places include midwifery and alternative birth settings, the so-called normal birth is defined by doctors' recommendations, which operate largely within hospital protocols (Sterk, Hay, Kehoe, Ratcliffe, and Vande Vusse, 2002).

Could postfeminism refer to the idea that all aspects of interpersonal relationships, including the most personal—that of touch—honor what is seen as womanly as well as what is seen as manly?

The facts do not bear this out. Research on touch and its role in human development shows distinctive gender-related differences. From the earliest moments of life, girls are touched more than boys but more gently, and boys are touched less than girls but with greater vigor. A balance between giving and receiving physical care seems to remain out of reach for both women and men.

Might a level playing field mean that women and men engage in sport on an equal basis?

Many would think they do. However, such is not the case. Even though women as well as men have played sports since the early 1900s in school, semi-professionally, and professionally, they are not equally involved in sport. Title IX notwithstanding, only 20.6 percent of the coaches of women's and men's teams in collegiate sport are women (Acosta & Carpenter, 2008).

Could postfeminism mean that management now emphasizes communication skills that once were associated with women?

Statistics indicate that as the managerial position takes on more status and pay, so, too, does the probability that a man holds the position. In the United States, for example, only 1 percent of the corporate executive officers of the Fortune 500 companies are women. Of Fortune 500's top earners, only 2.7 percent are women. About 11 percent of senior managers in the United States are women (Statistics–Women, 2007). Low as this is, this percentage is higher than that found in most other countries, including the Netherlands (Online Women: Statistics, 2007).

Paradoxically, seeming changes in gender relations only mask a substantial lack of change. These life paradoxes call for consideration of the reasons why gender relations remain structurally asymmetrical, with men and valued forms of masculinity continuing to hold the means of cultural control both literally and symbolically. What dynamics will need to change in order to crack and break the glass walls and ceilings of gender inequity?

PARADOXES AND TABOOS

One argument for the continuity of masculine gender hegemony prevails: the claim that gender differences are all just a matter of personal choice. If women really wanted to play sports, hold political power, and have active professional careers, they would have created opportunities for themselves and done them. This argument says that women really yearn to be mothers and homemakers—and when women go against these natural inclinations, they and everyone else suffer (Flanagan, 2004).

In Christian circles, potency is added to this argument by claiming that women and men were created by God to fulfill different destinies. Evangelical gender activist organizations, the Council for Biblical Manhood and Womanhood (The Council on Biblical Manhood and Womanhood, 2008) and Promise Keepers (Janssen & Weeden, 1994), suggest that men's destinies are to lead and women's are to be led. These organizations present gender differences as essential, created, or at least natural. Anyone who fights these differences is just asking for trouble. Another argument may seem more benign—as time passes, change will happen inevitably, so do not worry about it and try to force it ahead of its time. This is the point of view of author John Stackhouse in the Christian gender book, *Finally Feminist* (2005). Current inequities, he suggests, will fade away as a new generation takes this one's place.

It seems taboo to argue, in the midst of an apparent cultural movement toward equality, that cultural institutions are still patriarchal in nature and that the things associated with women continue to be devalued. Taboos make it hard to argue that meanings associated with *men* and *manly* still are valued more than those associated with *women* and *womanly*. The taboos are so deeply embedded that they may be all but invisible. It takes clear and subtle analysis to reveal them. In this book, we argue that the taboos need to be named and then transgressed in order to determine the deep culture of disrespect toward all that is associated with *womanly*. The differences in valuation of *womanly* and *manly* permeate people's sense of their own gender identities as well as meanings assigned to other people, events, and even ideas. Women's life potentials will remain stunted as long as they and men, too, believe they do not deserve equitable treatment in every aspect of life.

Paradoxes and taboos work together. Rhetorics of equality, equity, and postfeminism imply that gender and power analyses should be things of the past, yet women lag behind men in terms of cultural respect in almost every area of life. Paradoxes abound. The taboos that stop people from questioning these paradoxes keep people from rigorously challenging the dynamics of masculine hegemony. We will raise paradoxes and question taboos about gender in order to move thinking and action toward fuller realization of human potential and partnership. In doing so, the good of people in general will be served. Both men and women benefit when women receive cultural respect. As long as women and all that is symbolically associated with them are devalued, humanity itself is reduced. Both women and men become more fully human when their creativity and potential are recognized. People experience a wider range of behaviors when they are not constrained by the artificial (but effective) barriers of paradox and taboo.

The kind of communication and social work that needs to be done to break down paradoxes and taboos relies on motivating change. While powerful motivations for change in gender have come through legal means, such as the Lilly Ledbetter Fair Pay Act and Title IX, this book will argue that change also is motivated by a human desire to care for each other. As the introduction will show, care theory provides a useful heuristic for understanding how claiming, enacting, and holding on to our common humanity within strongly gendered contexts also motivates change. And we believe that the most persistent and tenacious movement toward change comes when people desire it, rather than are forced toward it. However, we also realize that the force of law often provides the initial impetus toward change. In this book, though, we explain meanings given to gender and how those meanings can promote good things in people's lives.

We are especially interested in exploring contradictory meanings given to human bodies in action, which we call "physicality." Physicality offers a particularly clear playing space for seeing and explaining gender identity, structures, and cultural meanings. When people think about gender differences, they often refer to the active body or physicality, such as giving birth or playing contact sport. However, physical necessity rarely motivates human actions, unless you are talking about birthing or breastfeeding. Instead, the *meanings* given to these differences, to being embodied as male and female and their lived-out consequences, incline us toward doing what we do. Analyzing the gap between cultural meanings given to 'physicality' and the respect or lack thereof assigned to 'womanly' makes up the spine of this book. We attend to meanings given to human bodies as they do particular things, in particular times and places. In doing so, we show that understanding people as human is more productive in terms of valuing the full capacities of people than categorizing them as male or female.

WHO ARE WE?

The two authors of this book bring divergent personal passions, life experiences, and professional training that allow them to do much more together than they can do alone. Annelies Knoppers, a sociologist of sport, has lived in Canada, the United States, and the Netherlands. Annelies researches and writes on the sociology and management of sport in both North America and the Netherlands. This project benefits from her experiences as an immigrant, athlete, researcher, and active church member. She brings to the topic of gender and physicality her love and rich knowledge of sport, including how it is practiced and made meaningful, as well as her training in feminist and sociological theory.

Helen Sterk, a rhetorician who takes gender as her primary subject, has lived in the United States and also for a short time in Hungary. Helen takes the topic of care and control as it relates to gender communication as her primary research focus. To this current project, Helen brings her experiences as a mother, an ethnographer of birthing, and an active church member, as well as her training as a rhetorician. Each experience helps her see life as integrated and complicated, not easily or meaningfully categorized and boxed.

Our many life experiences and professional training have prepared us to articulate the ways in which physicality and meaning come together. We first worked together in 1989–1990 as members of the group of Christian scholars that wrote *After Eden: Meeting the Challenge of Gender Reconciliation* (Van Leeuwen et al., 1993). We also share a long friendship with a healthy regard for each other's strengths and gracious forgiveness of each other's weaknesses. Our common professional ground lies in cultural analyses of gender. When we see broken relations, unfulfilled potential, and constrained lives brought about by distorted ideas of gender hierarchy, we look for ways to bring respect, healing, and wholeness to human beings. This is what we think of as 'gender justice.' Through understanding the paradoxes and taboos of gendered meanings as they affect the ways we live in our bodies, we believe re-formation can occur, leading to fuller life for all people.

WHAT IS DIFFERENT ABOUT OUR APPROACH?

Meanings motivate individual and collective action and vice versa. In terms of gender, particularly, meanings drive what people do. At each level of action, containment rhetorics operate like taboos, through explicit and implicit messages of shame or guilt if the rhetorics are violated. Containment rhetorics use real or implied threats and rewards to corral people into the boundaries of culturally 'appropriate' behavior, in this case, into bounded gender-appropriate actions. People interact with each other and negotiate the boundaries. At each level, people choose to reinforce, contest, or alter the messages given to them—people make decisions, always against the backdrop of what is seen as possible or ideal. Sometimes they go along with the containment rhetoric; sometimes they challenge it; and sometimes they just change it completely.

This approach is in contrast to two other currently popular approaches. One looks at the human body as enacting gender in given ways because of its physical and chemical makeup, which can be seen as an essentialist understanding of gender. Many popular writers on men and boys who say that testosterone drives males and trying to go against it is useless (Gurian, 1997, 1999; Sommers, 2001; Tiger, 2000), tap into this approach, which depends on a naïve acceptance that biology is destiny. The other approach, a performative understanding of gender, assumes that all meaning is created by individuals who choose just what to do in their personal performance of gender (Butler, 1993, 1999; Duncan, 1996). In other words, the first approach takes as a given that human gender is hardwired into people and, therefore, should be honored in the way we behave. The second argues that gender is more like software, and, therefore, is found in a set of choices made by each individual as she or he lives life. We find both points of view to be reductive. The one reduces humans to bodily structure and chemistry; while the other ignores the communal and communicative aspects of gendered life. While our biology *influences* certain aspects of our lives, such as whether our bodies allow us to bear children, it does not *determine* us. Humans make choices and the choices we make are based on the meanings we construct.

We believe that the truth lies somewhere in between hardware and software, those two reductive senses of how humans live out gender, in a space that honors both individual humans and communal living. While there may be givens in human female and male bodies, such as the ability to produce eggs or make semen, these givens by no means determine the full potential of someone's life. In response to the idea of gender as performance, we recognize the existence of physical boundaries that affect some performances as well as socially and culturally constructed boundaries. Our position is that individual human bodies are created with potential for life. No one fully lives out their physical potential, but often people do more than they think or have been told is possible. People often surprise themselves (and others). The gendered meanings that people hear and see and internalize can limit but also can encourage. Therefore, in this book, we look at the intersections of physical givens, social and cultural meanings, and individual performances.

We do so by analyzing and evaluating societal meanings with the use of discourse analysis and by focusing on human physicality in motion and action. This means that we will look at physicality as it takes place in a variety of contexts, including homes, schools, hospitals, businesses, and sport, to show the gendered meanings that are given to the human body in motion, exploring how those meanings affect human choices. In order to ground this study, we have chosen a series of topics that explore gender and physicality: giving birth, relating to one another through touch, sport as a context for gender play, and how physicality permeates the professional context of business management. We have chosen several specific life contexts for our analyses because we believe they best allow us to show how societal meanings operate—how people in the processes of moving, living, interacting with others, and presenting themselves in private and public life both react to and create gendered meanings. People act and react in certain ways because of the meanings they believe actions carry. Meanings lie at the core of reasons for action. In terms of gender, meanings drive what people do.

Containment rhetorics emerge in the dominant discourses of life. When people expose these dominant discourses, deconstruct them, and hold them up to view, we can deal with them. Once those discourses and their limiting forces are recognized, we can change them; their power is shared, broken, or transformed.

Creative methods are required to bring this all to life. Showing how paradoxes and taboos operate calls for concrete explanation, not just theoretical talk. We will use people's stories in these chapters to put flesh and blood into talk that can feel categorical and abstract. The stories and examples we use come from a variety of cultures, but particularly American and Dutch, not only because that is what we know best but also because their gender norms differ in interesting ways. Our method will draw on comparison and contrast in order for us to be clear.

REFLECTIONS

Our final goal will be to tell the stories of physicality, gender, and culture in such a way that readers will be able to see dominant discourses within several key life contexts and that readers will be equipped to respond to these discourses and others like them in their individual lives as they interact with institutions, and as they enter into their own symbolic meaning-making. We wish to open a space for discursive gender practices that bear a distinctive stamp in which creativity, stewardship, and encouragement of each one's gifts and talents within the context of communities take priority. We aim to show that the full colors of humanity cannot be seen until all that is associated with womanly is valued as highly as all that is associated with manly. We hope this book will help readers learn more about the influences that operate in their lives and use that knowledge to help them seek full, authentic lives for themselves and others.

Finally, we want to thank the people who helped this project come to completion. At Lexington Books, Jessica Bradfield offered invaluable support and advice. Lexington's reviewer gave encouragement and advice that shaped the final manuscript in crucial ways. And at Calvin College, the people of the Calvin Center for Christian Scholarship, especially directors James Bratt and Susan Felch, enabled this project through their financial support, which allowed the co-authors to consult with each other in person, even though an ocean separated them. The Calvin College Communication Arts and Sciences Department's special fund supported the final copysetting work of the book. Thank you, all of you, for the care you showed for us.

INTRODUCTION

During World War II, when so many American men were at war, a market remained for baseball. In order to feed a continuing appetite, the so-called great national pastime mutated overnight from a man's game to a woman's game. When the men came home, they could again be the players and fans. Until then, the game needed to continue. As a result, league owners recruited women to play baseball. The film, *A League of Their Own* (Marshall, 1992) chronicles the story by showing how the paradox between an emancipatory and a containment rhetoric operated for these women athletes, a rhetoric that encouraged the perception of them as outstanding athletes but coaxed the players into displaying skirt-wearing femininity, thereby containing their athleticism. A complex web of paradoxes and taboos grew around the women's baseball league so that the women and their play would be interesting enough to maintain the fan base but not usurp men's baseball and could be removed from active play when the war was over.

The main paradox was that the players had to meet a professional male-defined standard of athleticism on the field (while dressed in skirts!), yet not enact masculine behavior off the field. After all, these were women! Their ball playing required a feminine look. Thus, even though they played the same game as the men, with a hard ball, sliding in to steal bases or home, moving the game along at a fast pace, they were required to look and act like ladies. If they were great ball players, but looked a little too masculine, that edge had to be softened; they had to wear skirts and attend charm school. When the men came home from the war, the women's league slowly died. Women's professional baseball then went the way of women's welding and industrial jobs (Cahn, 1994; Field, 1999).

This example shows how gendered meanings inflect human action. Both men and women can play baseball. It is altogether possible that they could play it in the same way, wearing the same clothes, and meeting similar standards of excellent play. However, when masculine privilege, feminine subordination, masculine and feminine styles, and economic dynamics met on the playing field, the culture of women's baseball had to be reshaped so it did not look like a men's game. When the perceived need for men to retake their place in sport kicked in after the war, women had to move out of public playing space. In this example, as in so many others, neither physical necessity nor biological differences caused men's professional sport to triumph over women's. Instead, a power-filled set of economic practices and cultural discourses brought about the end result.

This sort of complicated enactment of gender discourses and practices provides endlessly productive material for analysis and ideas for meaningful change leading toward gender equity, in which people enact their humanity fully instead of just their gender. In this chapter, we will define terms (such as discourses, gender, physicalities, femininities and masculinities, and gender equity) and explain the bases of the analyses of birthing, interpersonal relationships, sport, and management that will make up the rest of the book.

Primarily, we will explore and analyze gender paradoxes and taboos through straightforward comparison and contrast. Using cross-cultural, historical, and situated analyses, we will show how seemingly common-sense ideas about gender actually are products of times and situations. We mine these analyses of birthing, sport, touch, and management for strategies for transformative action that will enhance cultural respect for what is associated with women, moving toward a new understanding of *human* that includes women every bit as much as men. In brief, we aim to develop a clear understanding of possible discourses and practices that could enhance gender equity in society and culture.

DISCOURSES AND PRACTICES

What does it mean to live out expectations for a certain type of gender, for example, masculinity? In some contexts, in addition to certain biological distinctions, masculinity could entail intellectual achievements;

in others, being physically dominant; in yet others, being financially successful, or a combination of all of these. The meanings and expectations given to manly behavior depend on a variety of situations, including how people interact with each other in different contexts, whether that be European or African, academic or business, political or religious. However, in any situation, when men, and even women, behave in ways labeled as womanly, they risk cultural disrespect.

In cases of gender performance, both definition and evaluation enter in. Definition and evaluation both depend on *discourses*: things that are written, said, and pictured about a given topic. By talking or writing about social objects, people give them meanings. In politics, this is known as "spin." Discourses and their implicit subtexts put a spin on meaning. Through persuasive subtexts, discourses let people know what can and cannot be said (what is and is not taboo) and what will and will not be allowed. Within a culture, people learn through discourses how life should be. Discourses carry powerful, ideologically loaded messages about what counts as truth, commonsense, and appropriate behavior within the context of the message (Kiesling, 2005; Whitehead & Barrett, 2001). Within a culture, discourses are found in both elitist and popular low culture, from books and pulpits to advertisements and television series.

Although many meanings may coexist for a given topic, a few will emerge as *dominant discourses*: certain meanings become dominant and imbued with power. Discourses become dominant and seen as 'truth' as they are repeated across media, over time, amongst people, and as certain social groups benefit from them. Consciously or unconsciously, people take hold of meanings and use them to explain events that happen, thereby reducing the uncertainty of life and serving as scripts for action. For example, when the president chooses to go to war and it is presented as a stand-up, manly act, a country may go along with it whether that meaning is right or wrong. As different media repeat the theme of manliness that becomes associated with this decision, the positive aura of masculinity can protect the president from backlash for the decision. However, if the dominant discourse moves from one that plays up the president's strength and manly resolve to one that highlights his rigidity and lack of masculine reason, earlier praise of his actions could change to criticism. In both cases, the positive value of masculinity remains the same, even though the action to which masculinity is attached may change.

Through *discourse analyses* such as this, we see the processes by which certain discourses become dominant, how they change, and how others are marginalized. What we see can be understood, and what we understand can be changed.

The actions of many people are usually based on embedded meanings so that their actions coexist with discourses. These actions, known as *discursive practices*, reinforce the power of dominant discourses. For example, in the 1950s and 1960s, the dominant discourses of gender, from advertisements to *Leave it to Beaver* to *Look* and *Life* magazines, showed men working outside the home for pay and women taking care of the home for no pay. For many people, discursive practices followed the dominant discourse—moms stayed home and had babies, contributing to the baby boom, and dads worked in business and industry. There were, however, many invisible exceptions. Over time, more and more women entered the paid workforce, and men took on more domestic responsibilities. New thinking nudged *alternative discourses* about men's responsibilities for children and about women's suitability for the paid workforce into new and alternative practices. These *alternative practices* influenced dominant discourses, and vice versa.

These terms, *discourse, dominant* and *alternative discourses*, and *discursive practices*, point to the ways in which gender definitions make their way into real life. Gender definitions are created and formed by talk, writing, and images that enact, inflect (exaggerate in the dominant direction), contest, or subvert (turn on their heads) dominant meanings. When people engage in conversation in their work, home, schools, and churches; read the current best-sellers; and watch advertisements, television, and film, they interact with meanings which flow between people and cultural messages, mutually influencing each other.

GENDER, MASCULINITIES, AND FEMININITIES

Although people often think *gender* refers to women and that gender issues are women's issues, we define *gender* as a key category and practice for acting out culturally written scripts, which define privilege, power, and people's enactment of gender. There are many ways to talk about gender, such as gender identity (understanding oneself as man or woman, girl or boy, or transgendered), gender biology (in terms of chromosomes, hormones, body parts), and gender meanings. Gender meanings reflect how we act, talk about, and describe behaviors associated with gender identity. The words "masculine" and "feminine" often are used in this way. As we show throughout the book, these meanings are neither fixed nor universal. Instead, the definitions of what is considered "masculine" or "feminine" vary by setting, the physicality involved, and over time.

While common talk and practice treat gender as if it were the same thing as one's sex, that is, that men are masculine and women are feminine and that is just the way it is, gender more specifically refers to the historically and situationally located cultural and social meanings people give to *womanly* and *manly*. It is more accurate to think of gender as that which is associated with manliness and womanliness, or masculinity and femininity in a specific context, than that which is associated with categories of men and women. The later refer to human persons, with quirks and eccentricities and individualities, while masculinity and femininity refer to what is considered appropriate action for people in a specific context.

Discourse and discursive practices make up gender. The moment we choose words to describe someone's physical qualities, we are doing gender. The words we choose to name women and men are examples of ways of doing gender—bitch, witch, dyke, stud, waiter, waitress, and so on. The stories we tell about the differences between women and men construct gender categories, whether those be *Rocky*, *An Officer and a Gentleman*, or *Gentlemen Prefer Blondes*. Biblical figures such as Jacob and Solomon did gender by marrying several wives. When women choose to wear make-up and certain kinds of clothes or men dress in super-baggy pants that reveal their boxers, their practices reinforce or challenge dominant ideas or discourses about the ways in which men and women should act. A given culture's idea of gender should not be understood as natural (which might imply remaining the same over time and place) but as continually taking on meaning at both personal and collective levels.

No one person owns the meaning of gender; the societies, economies, cultures, and structures that we create and live within provide the meanings for us. The ways we live either contest or affirm those meanings. Gendered meanings imprint everything we do and how we do those things. They are part of us, our identities, and as such—created by humans—they also can be changed by humans.

Even a superficial consideration of gender and life shows that while there may be dominant messages about masculinity and femininity in a given culture, usually there are many ways to enact those two. The two almost always exist and take on meaning in relationship to each other. One of the key findings of gender analyses over time is that a specific way of doing masculinity holds more power and is more respected than femininity in almost every culture. This practice of masculinity carries hegemonic weight in a given culture; its authority is unquestioned and unspoken and is carried out through implicit and explicit threats, rewards, and privileges. One way to see this is to think of which of the two genders is the marked case (requiring a qualifier) and which the unmarked (the term stands alone). While the practice is currently fading, it has not been too long since the terms *doctor* and *lady doctor* or *lawyer* and *woman lawyer* or *president* and *woman president* have been routinely used to indicate that men are the norm and women are not. As this practice fades, it has led some to argue that we live in a post-feminist age, where sex and gender do not matter anymore. Yet, our analyses in this book will show that masculinity's privilege emerges, sometimes in what is not said because of taboos and sometimes in the paradoxical gendered binds we create or find ourselves in.

While a given culture's hegemonic, or most prized, forms of masculinity and the complementary form of privileged femininity are quite easily evident within cultures, there are also many other types of masculinity and femininity that are acted out and are not as evident. For example, working-class men and women may have discourses and practices related to what it means to be male or female that differ from white-collar men and women. Working-class discourses about masculinity may emphasize physical strength, something not nearly as necessary for the discourse of upper management. Other social relations, such as race and age, play a role in framing meanings. Variations among social statuses, ethnicities, and locations of women and men require us to recognize that there are multiple *femininities* and *masculinities*, not just one of each.

The ways in which discourses interact with discursive practices are gender issues whether at the individual level (how persons do and do not use their bodies, what they internalize as right or wrong about their bodies) or at a cultural level. A woman who chooses never to bear a baby or a man who never engages in or watches sports or a transwoman who acts feminine while living in a male body challenge gender definitions with those actions. One reason is that *physicality*, or the body in action, evokes meanings. Meanings are created and associated with and placed on bodies in motion. The meanings played out through physicality have taken on important roles in constructing gender. R. W. Connell (2000) argues "bodies are arenas for the making of gender patterns" (p. 12) so that "gender is a social practice that constantly refers to bodies and what bodies do" (p. 27). Because we traditionally talk and write about and picture men as physically superior to women, and as women have moved further and further into physical spaces once reserved for men (in discourses about exercise, weight training, and sport, for example), meanings that we give to physicality have become key sites of struggle for gendered meanings. As we shall show, these discourses about gender rarely are value neutral.

One very striking way that physicality has generated new gendered meanings is in understandings of masculinity. To assume that all men possess inherently unitary qualities of masculinity, and therefore are stronger and physically more skilled than women, misses the dynamic and ambiguous nature of lived experience among men themselves (Connell, 1987, 2005). Black men, for instance, may be subordinated as a general group, but outstanding black athletes, such as Michael Jordan, may also serve as exemplars of masculine physicality. To aspiring black and white players, Jordan may have served as an icon of upward mobility. Black men, though, could see Jordan as a particular example of black empowerment. For Chinese and Chinese-American men, basketball star Yao Ming takes on similar meaning. Each meaning depends on its context, including the viewers' own physical qualities, ethnicity, and social status. Each meaning thus reflects a facet of masculinity, suggesting there are multiple masculinities rather than just one.

Masculinities differ in status, power, and privileges. They play out in relation to other masculinities and also in relation to femininities. Meanings given to masculinities depend on labor relationships (who does which jobs and who assigns them), emotional relationships (who is allowed to love whom and who may show what emotions), on power (the ability to have influence within formal and informal structures), and on dominant cultural discourses (Connell, 2000). As a simple contrast, black men and gay men enact masculinities that are often marginalized or subordinated in white Western society. However, one thing remains constant for many, if not most, masculinities. They each carry what Connell calls a "patriarchal dividend" (2000). What that means is that, even as masculinities are different and distinct from each other, what they share is the subordination of women; the marginalization of other masculinities; and even if unequally, male-related privileges.

It is worth a closer look, briefly, at three specific dominant discursive practices about masculinity in order to see how these qualities play out. These three tend to reappear in definitions of what it means to be a man: male solidarity that often mobilizes collective masculinities, heterosexuality, and dominance (or control) (Kiesling, 2003; Martin, 2003). These three show a cluster of attributes that contribute to patriarchal privilege. "Male solidarity" refers to the preference that men often have for each other's company socially (also known as *homosociality*, not to be confused with homosexuality), are supportive of each other and shows up in designations such as the "good old boys club." This male solidarity tends to exclude those who do not fit based on the type of group and/or network defined by gender, age, race, and so on. In relation to sexuality, discourses about masculinity stress heterosexuality. The word 'masculinity' is often used as a synonym for heterosexual desire. For example, in response to a researcher's question about his personal definition of masculinity, a gay man replied, "Don't ask me; I'm not straight," (Knoppers & Anthonissen, 2004). Not being heterosexual, this man took it to mean he had no personal definition of masculinity because heterosexuality for him *meant* masculinity. The third discursive practice, dominance, equates masculinity with being in control of situations, things, and people. Showing vulnerability or weakness is often disciplined in men and boys by telling them to "stop acting like women/girls."

While these three discursive practices do not comprise the sum total of categories for defining and practicing masculinity, they come close. They overlap, sometimes contradict, and sometimes trump one another. For example, when a group of men are together, not all can be in control or dominant. Further, men's desire for women sometimes overwhelms their need for social engagement with men. At times, male practices attempt to accommodate several categories at once (as we shall see in the sport and management chapters). Finally, there may well be discrepancies between what a man says and what he does; discourse and practice may be out of sync.

When there is a difference between discourse and practice, that does not mean that discourses do not affect, or even predict, practice. Idealized images do shape and influence individual, collective, and institutional discourses. For example, a man may reject a macho masculinity style and say that this rejection means he refuses to conform to stereotypes. Yet, the rejection may actually enhance perceptions of his autonomy and independence, also qualities associated with dominant practices of masculinity (Wetherell & Edley, 1999). Similarly, as previously mentioned, men may draw on heterosexual discourses and still prefer the company of men to women (as was the case of the close male friend characters of Denny Crane and Alan Shore on *Boston Legal* [Kelley & D'Elia, 2008]). Resistance and complicity can coexist.

EQUITY, DIFFERENCE, AND CARE

It is very difficult to pin down meanings for masculinities and femininities. As soon as one tries, ambiguities, exceptions, and contradictions pop up. Whitehead (2002) observes that masculinity is a paradox, existing both as a biological illusion and as a social and material reality. Description evokes paradox, such as gay men who exhibit the hypermasculine muscularity that has been associated with heterosexuality. Still, the actions and words coming from people whose bodies appear to be male are attributed to masculinity.

Even though masculinity as an idea may be illusory and a thorough understanding of masculinities is impossible, what we can do is come to an understanding of discursive practices and discourses of and about them. Masculinities come about through the creation and play of plural, changing, and historically informed discourses. They emerge as meaningful stereotypes of muscularity, sexual and physical assertiveness, male bonding, competitiveness, concern for control, and aggression (Whitehead & Barrett, 2001). Even though not all men engage in or care about such behaviors, they still may profit from the patriarchal dividend and slipstream behind them. Thus they are complicit in the stereotypes (Demetriou, 2001).

What has been said here about masculinities can be said, too, for femininities. While there may be dominant discourses and practices, not all women choose to live by them. However, even choices that women feel they have come to freely, as was shown to be the case for men, are tinged with cultural givens. Thinking of gender as only a personal choice performance may seem attractive. Understanding women as individually choosing cesarean delivery or choosing to wear short, tight skirts or choosing to work for less pay than men at different jobs than men do or choosing to do gymnastics rather than wrestling is easier to accept culturally than the idea that women as a group are being discriminated against or may have relatively few choices. While such thinking may be easier, we believe it is wrongheaded.

In this book, we align ourselves with gender theorists, such as Francine M. Deutsch (2007) and Judith Lorber (2000, 2005) who call into question the idea that individuals freely choose how to enact gender. These theorists compellingly argue that the idea of doing gender added an important component to understanding human agency in gender relations, but that stopping at that point limits people's abilities to imagine change. Progressive thinking in understanding gender moves from thinking that gender is something people innately *have* (as do authors such as John Grey [1993], John Eldredge [2001], and Michael Gurian [1997, 1999]) to thinking it is something people *do* to understanding gender as something that can be *undone* (Deutsch [2007], Lorber [2000, 2005]). By thinking about gender as something that can be undone as well as done, options for change emerge. When people undo, resist, or challenge cultural notions of gender, those acts promote change.

This crucial point may be understood through an example. Researchers Benjamin and Sullivan (1996) studied how heterosexual couples of varied income and communication skills, of whom one was a woman who worked in a professional career, shared housekeeping responsibilities. They found that the women with the highest income and also the most well-honed communication skills (marriage counselors) were most successful at achieving equitable sharing of housework. Women with the highest income and the least developed communication skills (accountants) gained the least success in sharing work at home. Further, women with great communication skills, but low income, were not successful in negotiating shared homework. Benjamin and Sullivan drew the conclusion that both financial power and the ability to communicate a desire for equitable sharing of work in the home were necessary to bring about change (1996).

Undoing gender does not mean that we erase differences between women and men. Instead, it means that we implement gender equity, in which both women and men are deemed fully and equally human. In earlier feminist times, during the second wave of feminism in the 1960s and 1970s, equality was the goal. In the name of equality, some feminist theorists went so far as to argue for doing away with all sense of sexual or gender distinction, to the extreme point of turning childbearing over to technologies, rather than people, so there would be no sex-marked differences between women and men.

Equity stands as a different kind of goal. Instead of eliding difference, Lorber (2000) claims: "Taking the stance of gender equity, we recognize the physiological and procreative sex differences between females and males, and look for ways to make them socially equivalent" (Lorber, 2000, p. 86). Social equivalence requires valuing all human contributions to life, from childbearing and rearing to manual labor to art to business to sport and beyond, no matter whether that contribution comes from someone who is rich, poor, white, black, brown, gay, straight, bisexual, transgendered, female, or male. Lorber wisely notes: "Diminishment of gender as an organizing principle of institutions and everyday life would not turn women into men any more than it would turn men into women. It would rather degenderize the best—and the worst—qualities of people" (Lorber, 2000, p. 90). If humanity rather than femininity or masculinity served as the key social and cultural organizing principle, then a wider range of social and cultural scripts would open up to people.

This point of view, that people are best served by practices that enhance their humanity, their place within human community, rather than those which constrain them, resonates with feminist care theories, with an ethic of caring for people through opening up a wide range of choices rather than controlling them through constraining possibilities. Care theorists argue that enhancing human life by finding good ways to open it up to potentials is as much a part of being human, if not more, as is control, such as is seen in gender policing. Educator and feminist theorist Nel Noddings (1984) situates her argument for human connection in the phenomenology of learning. Communication theorist Julia Wood (1993) locates our deepest sense of humanity in the recognition of the need to give and receive care. And political theorist Joan Tronto sees dependence as something built into the nature of being human, something that simply is part of who we are, not something to be seen as "character destroying" (Tronto, 1993, p. 163), but rather something that can build character. A point of view based on gender equity, rather than gender polarity, moves analysis and action toward those things that bring out the deepest and best things in people.

Care theory can direct an ethic of care, a set of principles or touchstones for human behavior that can shape life-affirming and enhancing actions. Historian Gerda Lerner's five characteristics of feminist consciousness (Lerner, 1993), with a little ingenuity, can suggest qualities of caring actions, whose net result is greater humanity for all people, no matter what their sex or gender identity.

Lerner's five characteristics are, first, to be aware of living in a symbolically maintained system of power relations; second, to realize that everyone, including oneself, has some level of power within the system; third, to see others as engaged with oneself; fourth, to tell the stories of their own situations; and fifth, to develop a vision of mutual care and responsibility. Taken together, these five do indeed constitute an ethic of care, a set of guiding principles that integrate self-love with interdependence. (Sterk, 2008, p. 125)

These guiding principles allow fully for individual differences, communal awareness, and mutual responsibility.

In this book, we aim to stimulate creative conversations about gender equity. Through stories and examples drawn from people's lives, the various chapters work toward one goal: to understand how large social, institutional, and cultural processes work to construct gender and to present analyses of individual agency that call those constructions into question, and ultimately, move toward helping people value each other fully in all their humanity. Chapter one considers what birthing might look and feel like if women's humanity (with all its attendant needs, desires, rights, and privileges) took priority in decisions about care during pregnancy, labor, and delivery. The second chapter analyzes the impact of gendered expectations and assumptions on human touch, showing how those expectations and assumptions encourage actions that do not lead to human flourishing. In chapters three and four, we focus on the roles that gendered discourses and practices play in sport, both for men and for women. Chapter five extends analysis of the symbolic resources of physicality and sport into work, particularly into management. Each chapter attends to physicality as it plays out in social and cultural settings, showing both the constraints of contemporary constructions of gender and the potentials open to people when those limits are contested or resisted.

Given all the complexities of gender definitions, discourse, and practices, we make no claims to pin down the essences of masculinity and femininity so that we can offer advice about how best to live them out. Instead, through analyzing gender discourses in a variety of life contexts, we plan to show the complications of gender performance and suggest that there are ways to live that lead to more abundant life than can enacting hegemonic masculinity and privileged femininity.

1

BODIES GIVING BIRTH
The Gendered Politics of Birthing

And the thing that struck me, even in my disorienta-
tion and pain, was that it was a [delivery] room full of
people. There were people everywhere. I don't know
if they belonged there or were just passing through.
But they were all in green scrubs, and were all wearing
masks and hoods. So, I could sort of make out who was
male and female, but other than that, it was a room
full of strangers.

—Jane F., 1996, p. 7, on her first birth,
doctor-directed, in a hospital.

And she [the midwife] just said very calmly to me,
"Okay, now start pushing." And she would say, "Ok,
slow down, slow down." I felt like we were working together at it, that she was guiding it. She said, "Now you
are going to tear and I'm going to give you a little episiotomy." I'm thinking, "Oh shit, another episiotomy."
. . . She gets this tiny little scissors and goes "snip."
—Jane F., 1996, p. 14, on her second birth, midwife-
directed, in a birthing center.

Same woman, two very different birthing experiences. In the first,
Jane felt alienated, estranged from the people helping to bring her
baby into the world. In contrast, in the second, Jane relaxed into a part-

nership with her caregiver, feeling as if she were being guided rather than controlled. If birthing were a valued human experience, would it not make sense for it to look and feel routinely like the second example?

Giving birth may stand as the paradigmatic female action, one done exclusively by women. Of course, not every woman gives birth; women's value as human beings does not increase or decrease if they have birthed a child; however, many women do bear children and that matters. Life on earth depends on women bringing children into the world. Because only women give birth, there is no possibility of equality, which carries assumptions of sameness, between women and men in this act. However, principles of human equity that imply offering equal opportunity for flourishing might guide caregiving and women's agency in giving birth. An ethic of care might lead people to see why the actions in that first anecdote of birthing are less desirable than those in the second. If birthing were framed as a human activity, rather than a woman's, what would it look like?

The short answer to that question is that if people looked at birthing as something humans do, then women, caregivers, and institutions would focus on how best to serve the human needs of women who give birth. Minimally, those needs would include dignified and respectful treatment, careful listening, financial support to pay for any medical expenses, full inclusion of partners in the process, and recognition of different rhythms of the birthing process; in brief, an ethic of care (Carlton et al., 2005; Sterk, Hay, Kehoe, Ratcliffe, and Vande Vusse, 2002).

An ethic of care presumes the full value of all people and requires that time be taken to realize how best to honor people who are involved together in life situations. Honor for others shines through in the foundational principles and style of communication that a person practices. Operating on five basic standards, this ethic (1) calls for awareness of the symbolic power system within which one lives; (2) grants that all people within such a system have some degree of agency (or ability to make their meanings known and felt); (3) understands, deep down, that the good of all people is interconnected; (4) encourages people to tell the stories of their own lives, from their point of view; and (5) uses these insights to develop a plan for action that incorporates varied points of view.[1]

Even though this chapter tells stories of one of the most private and personal acts someone can do, giving birth, the ethic of care we will argue for is not private, but public. As Joan Tronto argues (1993,

2000), if caring is to become something done institutionally and not just within families, it needs to be seen as an act of citizenship, something seen as good, necessary and required of all, not of just some. This chapter will pull apart current birthing discourses and practices, showing places where an ethic of care emerges and submerges, where women are framed as human beings deserving of attention and not treated as women who need to be controlled. Focusing on women's own stories of their birthing experiences, drawn from *The Birthing Archive* at Marquette University, the chapter will highlight intersections of class, race, and gender in birthing care, revealing paradoxes and taboos in this most primal, intimate, and personal play of gender and sexuality—giving birth.

ENACTING HUMANITY WHILE DOING GENDER—UNDOING STEREOTYPES

By rights, because women do the work of giving birth, it seems reasonable, even commonsensical, that birthing discourses and practices should be defined in the birthing-woman's terms. However, typically, this is not so. The paradox of birthing is that the commonsense understanding of birthing, like the commonsense understanding of almost any other gendered activity, turns out not to be the case.

Even though women give birth, its management, locations, and meanings paradoxically remain heavily influenced by impersonal, scientific norms, as if birthing were a kind of technology and women were types of machines. In current birthing practices, technological and surgical interventions are seen as not only normal but also ideal. To escape those norms takes a tremendous amount of personal will for women who would like to have babies on their own terms. It takes political organization and capital for groups who would like women to own birthing as well as well-placed influence to move symbolic constructions of birth.

As discussed in the introduction, people's natural bodies are situated in a complex set of gendered discursive practices. In this case, while the action of bearing children is completed by women's bodies, the work of those bodies is anything but natural, especially in American hospitals. By natural, we mean unmedicated, progressing in its own time and rhythms, and cared for through physical guidance rather than medical or technological intervention. Indeed, birthing is far from distinctive for each woman who does it. Birthing has turned into gendered work, given shape and meaning by assumptions and norms derived from clinical trials and practices and stamped with a view of women as neutral, interchangeable vessels for babies, rather than by observations and interactions with actual women. One woman, reflecting on her prenatal doctors' visits, wistfully noted, "Sometimes, I wished the doctor had a little more time to really talk to me and answer my questions. You see, they do all the routine tests and check-ups, but they really don't take time to listen to the patient. Sometimes I felt I had questions and the doctor was going, 'Ok, ok, next one'" (Sandra C., 1996). Clinical and hospital protocols tend to take precedence over situated decision-making. Both research and interviews with women bear out this claim, as the following sections will show.

In the early twenty-first century, a typical story of birthing in the United States goes as follows: If a woman has private or business-funded health insurance, she will see a doctor routinely during the nine months of her pregnancy. Her doctor is a member of a group of doctors, any one of whom might be the person delivering the woman's baby, depending on who is on call at that time. If she has no insurance, she gets little or no prenatal attention. According to a comparative study of maternity-care programs in western Europe and the United States, in the States, "More than 20 percent of all pregnant women and an even greater proportion of minority women fail to receive early prenatal care. Twenty-five percent of women of prime childbearing age are not protected by either public or private health insurance" (Miller, 1987, p. 211). At each doctor's visit, if a woman sees a doctor before her baby is born, the doctor routinely checks the woman's urine, weight, and belly size, rarely taking more than fifteen minutes, including time for conversation.

During pregnancy, women often take some sort of birthing class. Some classes, such as Bradley, aim at helping a woman trust herself and tune in to her body during the birthing process. Others, such as Lamaze, focus on giving women tools to use to overcome or ignore their pain; they also teach women about hospital protocols. Often, Lamaze classes include hospital visits, with introductions to the surgical suite, in case a cesarean section should become necessary, and also to forceps and the vacuum-extraction machine used to pull a baby's head out if it should become lodged in the birth canal. One woman described the hospital tour she and her husband took:

My husband found out, just at the tour, that if he becomes argumentative that they would remove him because he asked, "What happens if
the doctor wants to do something and we don't want it done? What
happens then?" And she [the nurse] said, "If it's not an emergency, the
doctor will explain it to you but if it's an emergency, they'll do what they
need to do." "What if it's something we don't want?" and she said, "If
you become argumentative, we'll have security remove you," so he was
terrified. (Dana S., 1996)

This anecdote shows graphically how at least this nurse viewed the relative importance of individual preference in relation to hospital protocol.

When birth pains begin, many women go straight to the hospital,
especially if it is their first birth. What they do not realize is that the
clock starts ticking on them as soon as they walk through the door. If
their baby is not born, or very close to it, within twenty-four hours of
entering the hospital, protocol, based on the average length of labor,
demands that the baby be taken by cesarean section. Further, as soon
as they settle into a birthing room, hospital machinery becomes part
of their lives. Fetal monitors, either in the form of a belt wrapped
around a woman's midsection or a small spiral lightly corkscrewed into
the baby's head, keep track of women's labor pains—their strength,
duration, and frequency. These monitors inhibit women's movements,
making it difficult, if not impossible, for women to walk, take a shower,
kneel, rock, or adjust their position to cope with the pains they are
experiencing. One woman described the kind of technological impera-
tive that monitors bring with them: "And they hooked me up to a fetal
monitor, which was horrible because I had back labor. . . . So, with every
contraction, I had this incredible pain in my back, but the nurse would
say, 'Lie still. Lie still'—because what would happen if I would move, I
had to lie on my back and when I would move, the fetal monitor would
dislodge and the alarm would go off" (Jane F., 1996, p. 4). Thus, in order
to accommodate the technology of the fetal monitor, women remain
somewhat immobile in their beds.

Sometimes, women's labor slows or even stops. If that happens, medical protocols demand intervention. Interventions often take the form
of using either pharmaceutical (usually through the administration of
Pitocin) or medical means (breaking the bag of waters) of inducing labor. Pitocin, a medicine that intensifies labor pains, makes labor more
difficult for a woman to manage because it does not increase labor
pains incrementally, as labor itself does, but exponentially. One woman

described what happened to her, "So, they put an IV in and hooked me up to the Pitocin and that's when I lost control of the contractions. . . . In retrospect, I look back and think, if they had just left me on my own, sure I may have had another ten hours of labor. But, I would have felt better about more labor knowing I was in control of my own body, feeling more like I was progressing with it instead of having it just taken out of my hands" (Jane F., 1996, pp. 5–6). Inducing labor may speed up the birthing process but does so out of sync with the rhythm of a woman's own body.

During early stages of labor, in addition to women using the breathing and focusing exercises of Lamaze or Bradley training, caregivers may bring in various forms of anesthesia in order to reduce women's pain. The anesthesia could be a narcotic medication, such as Demerol, or an epidural, an injection of drugs into a woman's spine through a catheter inserted in her back. Epidurals can be as strong as an anesthetic, where sensation and feeling are deadened (allowing it to be used during cesarean surgeries), or an analgesic, where pain is reduced. According to the American Pregnancy Association, 50 percent of birthing women have epidurals given to them (Epidural Anesthesia, 2008, p. 1). With an epidural catheter in a woman's back, her movement is limited, often requiring her to stay in bed. After the baby is born, it may take several hours for a woman to be able to move relatively freely again. During the past twenty years, epidurals have become more sensitive, allowing a minimal amount of drugs to enter into a woman so that she still is able to push her baby through the birth canal. Previously, epidurals could be so strong that women could not push, thereby increasing the need for forceps, vacuum extraction, or cesarean delivery.

As labor progresses and the baby makes its way through the woman's body out through the birth canal (if the woman is able to carry out a vaginal delivery), the doctor may decide to cut a slit from the woman's vaginal opening toward her anus, a procedure called an episiotomy, to allow more room for the baby's head and body. More than one woman interviewed for *The Birthing Project* talked about how doctors sewed their episiotomy cuts to make a smaller vaginal opening after the birth than before, usually in the name of increasing male partners' sexual pleasure (Lee H., 1986; Jane F., 1996; and Dana S., 1996). Because the sutures may leave scars, and the vaginal opening may be made smaller, *women's* sexual pleasure often declines significantly after episiotomies.

Therefore, impersonal office visits, protocol-driven hospital practices, fetal monitoring, medical or technological inductions, and episiotomies routinely structure American women's experiences of vaginal birth. These practices reduce women's agency by removing decision-making from them and encouraging passivity and thereby reducing her sense of power within that situation. In an implicit bargain for reducing the amount of pain they may experience in labor and delivery, women give away agency and active participation in this important human action. Disengagement marks the usual hospital birth. Just as in any human activity, when a person gives away their engaged involvement, no matter what the reason, there ensues a state of reduced humanity.

Analysis of three specific and relatively normal American birthing practices shows the difference between protocol-driven or care-driven decision-making: inductions, episiotomies, and cesarean section deliveries.

Inductions

When a baby is overdue, or a woman wishes to schedule delivery of her baby (perhaps to fit into a short maternity leave from work or to accommodate other personal reasons), or she has been in labor for twenty-four hours with not enough progress, or a doctor wishes to speed up a delivery, the caregiver may choose induction. Inducing birth may be accomplished in several different ways, from the natural (nipple stimulation or sex with a male partner) to the pharmaceutical (Pitocin—a synthetic form of the hormone oxytocin, prostaglandin gel, or the controversial off-label use of Cytotec—misoprostol[2]) to the technological (using a Foley catheter to put pressure on the cervix—causing the release of prostaglandins or rupturing the membranes of the amniotic sac). While there may be solid reasons for inducing labor, ranging from severe preeclampsia, pregnancy-induced hypertension, death of the fetus, or excessively prolonged pregnancy, many are calling this common medical practice into question. Has it been overused?

Over an eleven-year span, labor inductions doubled from 9.0 percent in 1989 to 20.5 percent in 2001 (Glantz, 2003). This statistical increase cannot be explained through increased need for it or through better outcomes for babies and mothers. It has always been possible to induce labor and delivery through natural means, such as nipple stimulation or sex; medicines and technologies have also been available for many decades. Why, then, the increase in inductions? If new scientific evidence found that it accounted for better chances for success and satisfaction for mothers and babies, that could be a reason, but such is not the case. Indeed, scientific evidence shows that inducing labor does just the opposite; it decreases the possibility of an uncomplicated birth.

A research study done in the Netherlands (van Gemund et al., 2003), a land known for having 80 percent of its births handled by midwives at mothers' homes, showed induction to be significantly correlated with increased cesarean section deliveries. One reason may be that many interventions ensue upon induction. Caregivers gave induced women more medications for pain relief, drew blood from the fetuses' scalps for testing more often, and did more cesarean deliveries with induced women than with those whose births were progressing on their own terms. These women were not allowed to labor on their own schedules, with minimal invasions of their bodies (with all the attendant opportunities for infection that come with multiple vaginal checks). Instead, inductions contributed to many interventions all the way up to cesarean deliveries. Fifteen percent of women whose labor was induced underwent cesareans, compared with 1 percent of women whose labor was spontaneous (van Gemund et al., 2003).

If this is the case in the Netherlands, where birthing is seen as something normal and uncomplicated and home birth is the norm, how much more might it be in the United States? The ability to control the pace of birthing seems too great a temptation to pass up. In the States, where one in five women find the timing of their birthing managed by caregivers rather than their own bodies, doctors have lost sight of how unmanaged or minimally managed birthing might progress. In the 1980s, Barbara Katz Rothman, cross-cultural researcher of birthing practices, noted this problem, "Since physicians within the hospital always go from one intervention to the next, there is no place for feedback; that is, one does not get to see what happens when a woman stays in the first stage for a long time without her membranes being ruptured" (Rothman, 1983, p. 265). She recommends that caregivers take their cues from the women in front of them: Let them start birth on their own and finish it the same way, letting labor start and stop, rather than intervene in a process that could continue well enough on its own. Let the woman determine the timing of the labor—not hospital caregivers who move to induction, forceps delivery, or to cesarean sections if it stops, "as if without forceps the baby never would have gotten out alive" (Rothman, 1983, p. 268).

Episiotomies

Current rates of episiotomies in America continue to hover around 30–35 percent, much reduced from the close to 60 percent rate of the early 1980s (Hartmann et al., 2005; Thacker & Banta, 1983), even though research has found little benefit and much physical harm in this surgery to mothers. The harm includes a potential range of effects from the pain of the cut and the discomfort of stitches to ongoing sexual discomfort to rectal dysfunction and fecal incontinence (Weber & Meyn, 2002). In contrast, in the Netherlands, episiotomy rates in the 1980s came in at 8 percent (Thacker & Banta, 1983). Not all women bearing babies vaginally experience the same rates of episiotomies: younger women and women with private insurance receive episiotomies at a higher rate than older women and women with government insurance; doctors tend to give black women fewer episiotomies than white women (Weber & Meyn, 2002).

Doctors may favor this cut over natural tearing because it is easier for them to control with surgical technologies, such as scalpels and scissors, than a tear and also is easier to sew up. Episiotomies remain under the doctor's control and decision, allowing him or her to determine the manner of birth. Midwives tend to massage the perineal area, helping the vaginal area to relax and open up. The following excerpt from *The Birthing Archive* shows how these two different practices feel to the woman receiving them. During Jane's first birthing, the doctor cut her: "But he did a huge episiotomy. . . . While he was sewing it up, he said to C. [her husband], kind of jokingly, he said, 'Well, I put an extra stitch in for you.' . . . It was very tight and there was a lot of scar tissue. . . In my heart I don't think an episiotomy would have been necessary. It took two years to heal. I am still not the same" (Jane F., 1996, pp. 7, 9). During her second birth, the midwife massaged her (and after that proved not to open her up enough, the midwife gave her a small episiotomy—see the anecdote at the chapter opening). The massage felt significantly different, as did the small episiotomy cut: "At that point about a silver dollar size of her head was already poking through. What the midwife was doing at that time, she was massaging the opening of the vagina with oil. She had started that right after she broke the water. I could feel her. C. told me later on, because he watched it, it was kind of like, and I don't know how you would describe it, like putting on a latex glove. She just kind of eased the skin around the head of the baby as the baby came out" (Jane F., 1996, p. 11). The two practices differ sharply in the care given to Jane. In the first, the caregiver seems to lack any empathy with Jane (indeed, ignoring her and showing more concern for Jane's husband than for her), while the second shows recognition of Jane's emotional and physical needs.

Episiotomies, a typical American practice, could be described as female genital mutilation in that while it may make a smaller opening for a male partner's penis, thereby potentially increasing his pleasure, the scar tissue combined with reduced size of the vaginal opening decrease women's sexual pleasure. Another woman's story in *The Birthing Archive* shows how upsetting this can be. After getting what her doctor called "a love knot" (his term for reducing her vaginal opening after episiotomy) (Lee H., 1996, p. 8), Lee talked with him about the pain she experienced during intercourse, and he suggested she try to relax by drinking a little wine before sex. She finally got angry and stalked out of his office: "'What the hell does he know?' I've been married seven years. We're not talking about I need to relax a little bit. I'm not a nervous bride" (Lee H., 1996, p. 8). The practice of episiotomy does not lead to better sexual relations between women and men. If women are not happy during sexual intercourse, chances are their male partners are not happy either, so episiotomy cuts and scars end up serving no one but the doctor.

Cesarean Deliveries

In the ten years between 1996 and 2006, cesarean deliveries increased by 50 percent, from roughly 20 percent of all births in 1996 to about 30 percent by 2006 (Yabroff, 2008). Not only American doctors but also women view cesarean delivery as a reasonable choice, not only in the case of danger to the child or mother (such as certain breech presentations or placenta previa [where the placenta covers the cervical opening]) but also to reduce or bypass the pain of vaginal delivery.[3] "Too posh to push" (referring to an elitist attitude toward birthing labor attributed to celebrity Posh Spice) became a catchphrase in the early 2000s (Yabroff, 2008).

Whether through lack of knowledge or by choice, these points of view ignore the consequences of cesarean delivery. This major abdominal surgery takes about six weeks for full recovery, interfering with a woman's ability to lift and hold her new baby, and includes cutting through muscles, receiving stitches, and gaining vulnerability to infection. Women recover from normal vaginal deliveries far more quickly because there is less trauma done to their bodies. A study of the physical health and well-being of working women five weeks after giving birth found that vaginal birthing leads to better physical health and mobility than does cesarean delivery (McGovern et al., 2006). One woman interviewed for *The Birthing Project* described vividly her quick recovery from giving birth vaginally. She had her baby in Ontario, Canada, in the early 1950s. At that time, Canadian doctors had little exposure to natural birthing, which is relatively unmedicated and relies on the woman's body to do the work. Of the doctors, Emma V. said:

> But anyways, they watched my muscles actually. I was a little bit embar-rassed later. But they watched the muscles actually and they could see I could hold it and when the labor came, I could hold it and push it out. They could see the baby was moving and working with me actually, and they were so surprised and they were smiling. Oh, how was that possible, they couldn't believe, and then they said, "What are you doing now?" I said, "I can walk to my room." (Emma V., 1996)

She did walk to her room.

While not all women recover so quickly from vaginal delivery, many do. No one recuperates that quickly from cesarean delivery; abdominal surgery takes time to heal. Yet, cesarean sections account for one-third of the births in America. Henci Goer's mid-1990s comparative analysis of research presented in the *Journal of the American Medical Association* states that only about 15 percent of births are problematic enough to require medical intervention (Goer, 1995). Of those, not all require cesarean delivery but, rather, forceps or vacuum extraction. If we use a very conservative figure of 15 percent in reference to the number of labors that might suggest a cesarean delivery, current practices run twice as high.

Finally, unnecessary cesareans waste health resources. If a cesarean is medically indicated, it makes sense to bring in a full surgical team to support it. However, considering the resources that go into a cesarean: "a surgeon, possibly a second doctor to assist, an anesthesiologist, surgi-cal nurses, equipment, an operating theatre, blood ready for transfu-sion, if necessary, a longer post-operative stay, etc." (Wagner, 2001, p. 31), it is a poor use of resources to engage in unnecessary cesareans. Given the skyrocketing cost of medical care in the United States, it would be wise to save cesarean deliveries for emergencies.

Therefore, on a health policy as well as an individual level, it would make good sense to reduce rather than increase cesarean deliveries. Not only would women be spared the physical consequences of surgery, but health resources would be better used.

ETHNICITY, CLASS, AND GENDER IN BIRTHING: A CASE STUDY

Birthing, it seems, does not depend just upon the natural action of a woman's body. As the preceding section shows, cultural stereotypes of control and power shape women's own expectations of how birthing will go and the ways in which caregivers take choices away from them. Even when women believe they themselves have made an informed decision; for example, to schedule a cesarean delivery in order ostensibly to have a baby on their time and on their terms, that decision depends on internalizing a view that birthing itself does not matter—the baby alone does. The American way of birthing does not encourage women to see giving birth as a valuable human action—one they alone can do and that the way they do it matters. If women are to see themselves as human, as worthwhile, they will have to engage with the process of birthing, seek out caregivers who practice an ethic of care, and speak up for themselves. It is risky and hard in today's medicalized climate, but it can be done.

Consider the story of Sandra C., a Hispanic woman living in California, unable to afford private health insurance and who gave birth in circumstances described above but suffered complications after birth that required her to go against not only her doctor but also her husband and her mother in order to live. Sandra's dramatic story shows a woman who engaged with those who were in charge of the care of her body, perhaps not as much during the birth as after it. Her story highlights the significant costs of the lack of human agency—costs exacted when one is not considered fully human in the situation, which in her case came through in the ways in which people did not listen to her.

In the United States, one-fifth of women who bear babies receive no prenatal care from trained professionals (Miller, 1987). While Sandra did not fall completely into this category, prenatal care felt cursory at best to her. "I had a normal pregnancy, there weren't any complications; there weren't any big surprises or anything. It was just in my mind that I needed to have some attention. I wish the doctor who was taking care of me during my pregnancy would have taken care of me during labor" (Sandra C., 1996, p. 2). In the hospital where she gave birth, which was not the same one in which she received her prenatal care, three doctors and two nurses came and went during her labor, none of whom she recognized. She found herself in an unfamiliar place, with people she did not know, indeed, had not even met. In that context, she could not relax, could not let go. So, her labor slowed. In order to jumpstart it, the doctor ruptured her membranes, which speeded up her contractions faster than she could deal with them: "I was throwing up. I was feeling dizzy. I was drowsy, and just this horrible feeling of not being in control" (Sandra C., 1996, p. 3).

Because Sandra's contractions felt so overwhelming and painful, she also received an epidural, which relieved her pain but slowed down the contractions. Because her caregivers did not think her labor was progressing fast enough, they next hooked her up to an intravenous drip and gave her Pitocin. She said, "They do the epidural so you don't feel the pain, then you have to take this other medication so they can accelerate the contractions. Because the contractions got really slow again, it was like back to the beginning" (Sandra C., 1996, p. 4). As a consequence of her epidural, her ability to push effectively dropped. She said, "I was pushing, the baby was coming out, and the doctor was using that vacuum thing to suck the head" (Sandra C., 1996, p. 4). She told herself that the manner of the birth did not matter. "It really doesn't matter if I had the epidural or if I was trying to protect myself from the pain. That doesn't make you a better person or a worse mom. That's not the point of having a baby. The point of having a baby is watching over him, making sure he's fine, and taking care of him" (Sandra C., 1996, p. 5). Sandra's birth story fills the frame of a so-called normal hospital birth, complete with all the interventions except a cesarean delivery.

If Sandra's story stopped here, it would seem to reinforce the by-now-familiar narrative of the anti-care cooption of women's experiences in the name of protocol, normalcy, and routine. After all, nothing happened to her that had not happened to thousands or even millions of other women. Nothing new seems to be told in this story. However, what Sandra experienced after the birth of her child shows the extent to which women, especially Hispanic women and women without private insurance, receive inhumane treatment.

After Sandra's baby was born, she contracted mastitis, a painful inflammation of the breasts. Her doctor told her, "[t]hings like this just happen" (Sandra C., 1996, p. 6). Because her mother had come up from Mexico to stay with Sandra and her husband while they got used to their new baby, Sandra was able to rest a bit, but she did not get well quickly. Instead, the symptoms intensified. In addition to mastitis she had diarrhea and chalked it up to food poisoning but told her mother to call 911. Her mother was reluctant, believing that Sandra only had a stomachache. Sandra insisted and her husband took her to the emergency room in the hospital where she had received her prenatal care, not the one where her baby was born.

At the hospital, the doctor who saw Sandra gave her a pelvic exam, took blood samples, and told her that she had a pelvic infection—nothing unusual after giving birth and that she should take some antibiotics. Sandra went home, took the antibiotics, and kept feeling sick. Again, she asked her mother and husband to call 911 and again they resisted, encouraging her to let the medicine run its course. She fought for her life: "If you don't call 911 now, I don't think I'm going to live through the night. My mom got up and [my husband] called 911. I was taking a shower. When I was taking a shower I was crying because I wanted to take care of my baby. I wanted to watch him grow up. I didn't know why, but I was scared to die at the time. And I said to [my husband], 'The doctor is wrong'" (Sandra C., 1996, p. 6). Shocked, her husband protested, "How could that be, he's the doctor and he knows" (Sandra C., 1996, p. 6). When the paramedics came, they did not want to take her to the hospital because they thought the antibiotics needed more time to work. So, they left.

The next day, Sandra had her husband take her to the hospital where she had her prenatal care and told the doctor she was there for a follow-up check-up on her abdominal pain. The doctor said it was just a pelvic infection and she should go home, but Sandra insisted, "Well, I will stay" (Sandra C., 1996, p. 7). The next morning, a new doctor came in and said, "This is not a pelvic infection, these are the usual symptoms of appendicitis." They called the surgeon and the surgeon said, "Yeah, this is definitely appendicitis; this is not infection. If you don't have an operation right now, I don't know how to tell you this, but this is an appendix and it has ruptured, and something's going to happen to you" (Sandra C., 1996, p. 7). This happened one month after her baby was born. She said, "Thirty days after he was born, thirty days after I felt this wonderful feeling of happiness of having him in my life, I felt that I was going to die and have to wait for him in another place" (Sandra C., 1996, p. 7).

During the operation, the doctors took out the ruptured appendix as well as one of Sandra's ovaries because the infection destroyed it. As a result, Sandra feared she would never be able to have another baby. In spite of that fear, she had an intrauterine device put in for birth control. Even so, she got pregnant again: "Yeah, they took it [the IUD] out right away. I was four weeks pregnant when they took it out. When they took it out it was halfway out. It was probably the reason I got pregnant. My own body was rejecting it. I feel that after all I went through, it's a gift. It's something that somebody else up there wanted to happen. That's the story. That's what happened to me" (Sandra C., 1996, p. 8).

Sandra's story reflects themes of alienation and control by caregivers and personal resignation to her own lack of agency, themes common to many other women. Research on Hispanic women and birth shows that her story intersects with other Hispanic women as well. Distinctive among ethnic groups in America, Hispanic women's experience strongly displays cultural impacts on birthing, which generally means their birthing outcomes are better than women of other ethnicities (Albrecht et al., 1996). Available research does not argue why that is the case. It just presents those outcomes as the case. Clues from Sandra's story suggest a supportive family structure, especially the presence of her mother, and a strong sense of self, seen in Sandra's willingness to contradict her mother's and husband's trust of medical authority, may provide resources of care for Hispanic women.

For one thing, Latin American women's newborn babies tend to weigh more than babies born to white women: "No clear factors explaining the paradox were apparent, but Latinas may eat more nutritious diets and benefit from social and cultural advantages favoring healthy pregnancy and birth" (Fuentes-Afflick et al., 1999, p. 147). The presence of Sandra's mother in her home before and after the baby was born may represent one of those advantages.

Further, although this may be a mixed blessing and one perhaps related as much, if not more, to class and level of insurance than to ethnicity, a late 1980s study found that women who lived in areas of Los Angeles County where the median income exceeded $30,000 a year had a cesarean section rate of 23 percent, while women who lived in areas where the median income was under $11,000 had a 13 percent rate (Gould, Davey, & Stafford, 1989). Paradoxically, in this case, being poor may present a benefit in that it protects women from unnecessary cesarean deliveries. Generally, medical interventions in birth tend to increase where income or insurance can pay for them.

Finally, the most striking finding related to Mexican-born Sandra's case is seen in a study that found Hispanic ethnicity, particularly Mexican, related significantly to poorer quality hospital care, often leading to an unnecessarily high level of health complications: "Mexican-born women were significantly less likely to have one or more maternal morbidities [ailments or diseases short of mortality] than White, non-Latina women but more likely to have complications that reflect the quality of intrapartum care [care given during labor and delivery]" (Guendelman et al., 2005). The researchers do not speculate why that might be the case, whether economic status, language barriers, or what. However, we see in Sandra's story, over and over, her being ignored or patronized by caregivers who downplayed her knowledge of her own body. In the story, only one person seems really to see her, the doctor who recognized her symptoms as being those of appendicitis.

VALUING HUMAN BIRTH WORK

Sandra's story allows us to return to the question: "What would a fully human birthing situation look like?" If a woman were treated within an ethic of care, how would that affect her treatment during pregnancy, labor, and delivery? First, she would become well informed about the ways in which doctors and hospitals conduct birthing. She would also discover alternatives to a medicalized birth, such as free-standing birthing centers and midwives. Second, she would act as Sandra did when her life was threatened—take responsibility for her own choices and demand that she be heard. Ideally, this would happen all along the way, not just at the point of a severe threat to life. Third, caregivers and birthing women would partner together to make the birthing experience as positive as it can be, realizing that partnership serves women, caregivers, and babies better than unilateral control. Fourth, caregivers would listen to the stories people tell of their own lives. In the case of birthing, this would entail giving as much credence to women's stories as to hospital routines, thereby granting some authority to women about their own embodied experience. Finally, care plans would depend on the mix of research findings, women's narrations of their experiences, and caregivers' observational and experiential expertise rather than caregivers' need for control.

Medical doctor and birthing researcher Marsden Wagner contrasts such care, which he calls "humanized" with what he terms "medicalized" care, arguing for treatment to take women into account (Wagner, 2001). He joins the World Health Organization in recommending that "birth be controlled, not just by individual doctors and hospitals but by evidence-based care monitored by the government"[4] and give back birth "to the woman and her family" (Wagner, 2001, 26). This sort of birth enhances the work of women's bodies, minds, and emotions rather than overriding it by superimposing external forces and technologies on women. For him, human birthing would be best conducted outside of hospitals, in alternative birthing centers, located close enough to a hospital for emergencies, guided by midwives rather than doctors, and marked by collaboration between doctors and midwives rather than the current animosity toward midwives evidenced by doctors (Wagner, 2001, pp. 36–37).

Contemporary popular culture shows some pushback to medicalized birthing. Naomi Wolf urges women to speak up about their feelings, needs, and experiences—to stand up for themselves: "Not only are we inadequately informed about what pregnancy, birth, and new motherhood really involve, we also lack freedom to describe what we have seen for ourselves along the way" (Wolf, 2001, p. 2). Celebrity Rikki Lake allowed her water birthing to be filmed in *The Business of Being Born* so that women could see how well a minimally invasive, self-timed, and defined birth could work (Epstein, 2008). When celebrities share their positive experiences and points of view in these ways, ordinary people see role-modeling that can counteract the attitude of not only acceptance but also the embrace of medicalized birthing expressed in the "too posh to push" mantra.

In giving birth, women affirm the value of human life. Their bravery deserves respect. Too often, in the United States, women's role in birthing seems to disappear in the emphasis on doctors, hospitals, erasure of pain, and the safety of the baby. While all these matter, women's courage and agency should be uppermost in the minds of all involved in helping babies to be born. This distinctively human action should be honored with care that supports and endorses women's decision-making. That means an ethic of care should pervade the homes, birthing centers, and hospitals where birth takes place; that a full range of alternatives should be available to women; that birth be supported financially for all people; and that birthing women be heard.

CHAPTER 1

NOTES

1. For further development of how an ethic of care operates in gender contexts, see Sterk (2008). I derived this five-part ethic from Gerda Lerner's five criteria for feminist consciousness (1993).

2. Misoprostol, used under the name of Cytotec, was developed to treat ulcers. Because it is a type of prostaglandin, many obstetricians use it for its "off-label" effect of stimulating labor contractions. However, the drug's label explicitly warns not to use the drug on pregnant women because its use can rupture their uteruses (Wagner, 2003; Cytotec, n.d.).

3. For further insight into attitudes toward cesarean section as a choice, see the blog, "Healthy pregnancy: C-Section by choice" (2006).

4. Wagner argues that obstetricians tend to rely more on their experiences and anecdotes from colleagues than on research findings. Wagner's insistence on evidence-based decision-making would lead doctors to research findings that suggest, for example, that episiotomies tend not to be necessary, that cesarean deliveries should be avoided, and increased rates of inductions have not led to better birth outcomes for mothers or babies (Wagner, 2001).

2

BODIES IN TOUCH

Gendered Taboos

When six-year-old Katie broke her arm while bracing for a fall on a trampoline, her parents took her to the emergency room where a dedicated young doctor manipulated the bone to get it back in place so he could set it. Katie had learned her lessons on physical touch well. Over and over she screamed, "You cannot touch me! You are hurting me! This is bad touch! You are not my doctor! Leave me alone!" Relatively unperturbed, the doctor continued until Katie's arm was stabilized, enduring the curious looks of the nurses and other patients passing by. On the one hand mortified, but on the other proud of her assertiveness, her parents apologized for her outburst but smiled anyway.

One of the first things children learn from parents or day care or kindergarten is the difference between good touch and bad touch. They learn that good touch is something they are okay with. On the other hand, bad touch hurts them. It may be violent or sexual. In either case, bad touch is not wanted. And the children learn to say no to someone who uses bad touch on them. As simple and dualistic as the idea of good and bad touch is, to categorize touch this way carries over into adult life. However, what counts as good or bad becomes far more complex as gendered meanings of touch, with their connotations of sexuality and power, come to be understood. Once frightening, sexual touch turns from something that is fearful to something that is desirable. Once just fine, as when a parent guides a child learning to ride a two-wheeler, patronizing touch reaches a point when it is no longer welcome. Part of growing up depends on learning the codes of touch—those nonverbal codes that depend so much on context and relationship for meaning, especially in relation to gender.

In this chapter, we build on the previous one. Just as in birthing situations, meanings given to touch are affected deeply by culture, context, relationship, personal history, and observers as well as institutional and cultural tradition. Further, much of the content of media, including film, television, and music, depends on depicting touch in order to move the narrative, to motivate actions, or to indicate relationships. This means that, at the symbolic level, touch takes on rich and varied meaning and value. Part of being fully human is being able to touch and be touched in meaningful ways that enhance one's own life, as well as others' and to have the power to set appropriate boundaries for touch, not only personally but also in social and cultural discourses. This is the kind of touch endorsed within an ethic of care. It honors a person's right to choose how to be treated, communicates both respect and affection, and takes place within a culturally coded context. Knowing how the coded context works helps people make decisions about how to live.

A particular focus of this chapter will be on the role of touch in the lives of people who are raising infants, thereby allowing an argument about how people can use touch to create independence and self-reliance in girls and boys through a lot of good touch early in life. Learning about the complexities of human touch and acting appropriately on that knowledge enriches life, society, and culture, thus enabling one to live an abundant life.

MEANING AND TOUCH

How is meaning created? One useful approach to understanding this is through viewing communication as a type of speech act (Austin, 1975; Searle, 1999). Speech act theory suggests that the best way to understand how meaning is created, is to see meaning as emerging through a negotiated interaction of people in literal, social, and cultural situations. Through communication, people try out messages until there is at least a roughly equivalent understanding among the communication partners about the definition, interpretation, and value of some event. Personal experience mediates and affects the meaning of personal experience in complex ways. This includes gender, in this chapter referring mainly to *gender identity*, one's sense of one's own masculinity or femininity and *gender schema*, culture's script about what it means to be women or men and girls or boys.

Gendered meanings, influenced by culture, tradition, and personal experience, cluster around touch. These meanings have to do with power, not simply with individual differences among the ways in which women and men use touch to communicate. As in almost all of life, gendered meanings infuse people's sense of appropriate touching. No one person can determine the meaning of a certain touch. That meaning comes about through interaction and response. For example, when a boss touches an employee, the impact differs significantly from touches between friends. Bosses are empowered culturally and socially to touch the people who work for them. Reciprocity is not encouraged. Further, in a certain sense, the power difference operates whether or not the boss is male and the worker female. Yet, the effect of the touch depends to an extent on whether the person in power is male or female and whether the touch is same sex or opposite sex. Sexuality and power mix together in the meaning of touch in many other contexts, too, not just in work relations.

Thus, whenever there are two or more people, there also are context, relationship, personal history, and observers as well as institutional and cultural traditions. Add to this mix the ways in which media depicts touch. At the symbolic level, touch takes on rich and varied meaning and value. Those meanings always are situated within a cultural context—for good or ill. No one can separate themselves from its influence.

THE ROLE OF TOUCH IN PEOPLE'S LIVES

Nonverbal communication carries much of the meaning created among people. Some communication scholars have argued that from 65 to 93 percent of the meanings people take up in social life come from nonverbal communication (Birdwhistell, 1970; Mehrabian, 1981). These meanings are not so much about specific content as they are about the qualities of relationships among people (Keeley & Hart, 1994). In particular, messages of support, liking, responsiveness, and control are carried nonverbally (Mehrabian, 1981). In other words, nonverbal communication, such as touch, communicates *about* communication; it metacommunicates.

The more sophisticated someone's ability to discern those messages becomes, the more they come to understand other people; the status of the relationship; and, subsequently, how they are seen by others. In a good and perfect world, that new level of understanding meanings and how they are constructed and maintained would bring about better relationships and more loving involvement with others. However, given the human tendency toward distorting good gifts, including that of touch, many times people knowingly touch other people or withhold touch in order to harm that person through an undermining of a sense of support, which communicates dislike, limits warm response, and exercises inappropriate control.

As human beings, we are created to give and make meaning. Not all those creations or meanings are good and healthy. Two themes underlie the four functions of nonverbal communication set out by Mehrabian (1981)— the themes of sexuality and power. Both are sources of tremendous good and temptation for evil. Because of the power of these two, people need to be aware of the way they touch others and allow others to touch them. Further, they need to be able to analyze accurately what is being communicated through touch in order to be able to weigh people's intentions and evaluate the truth of people's uptake. These skills help to sort out what is implied or real violence, sexual abuse, sexual harassment, and sexually and powerfully inappropriate from what is not. Awareness and analysis of the speech act of a particular touch is a tool that can enable someone to name and perhaps to stop abusive situations. Because touch is also the source of great good, awareness and analysis can lend one the strength to continue with good touch, even in the face of social or cultural criticism. These cultural skills draw an ethic of care through analysis and understanding of touch. Naming abusive situations as such grants power to those who need it by giving them a tool to use to stop abuse. And knowing and talking about what is healthy for people allows the good to grow. Language provides the means to create a mutually satisfying situation of care and responsibility.

In the next section, we will analyze the individual, institutional, and symbolic meanings given to touch in infancy, adolescence, and adulthood, tracing the interrelated effects of sexuality and power on those meanings, thereby unpacking the ideas named above.

THE ROLE OF TOUCH IN INFANCY

From the earliest moments in a person's life, touch communicates something meaningful about the quality of relationships. Touch may be the first sense to develop (Leathers, 1976, 1986), and it is necessary to human thriving. When babies experience touch, the stimulation promotes them to gain weight and reduces their stress and postnatal health complications (Caulfield, 2000). Further, when the touch is nurturing, i.e., gentle, soft, and sustained, babies develop more secure attachments with their caregivers (Weiss et al., 2000; Weiss & Goebel, 2003). This sort of touch not only enhances bonding but, through the bonding, develops children's cognitive capacities and also their own caring behavior (Perry, 2002). Those very early experiences with touch carry over into the rest of life, affecting the meanings people give to touch and having an impact on the choices people make in relation to touch.

One vivid example shows the extent to which touch early in life affects a person's emotional development. David and Holly Meyers, who had adopted a seven-year-old boy from Romania, found to their sorrow that they had to reverse the adoption decision because the boy posed a danger to the mother and their other child. He not only brutalized the daughter but threatened to kill both the mother and daughter so that he could be alone with the father. The boy suffered from reactive-attachment disorder (RAD), a disorder marked by an inability to form close emotional bonds due to the complete lack of loving (or perhaps any) touch early in his life. From birth to age two, he was tied up in his orphanage crib. This disorder created a deep insecurity in him and a desire to remove anyone who got in the way of what he wanted (Agar, 2004). If this child had been held, cuddled, stroked, tickled, and played with by people with loving intentions from his earliest life, most likely, he would have escaped the deep emotional damage that he suffered.

Gendered constructions of meaning begin practically at the moment of birth, not only through parental practices but also often mediated through medical institutions. In America, if the baby is born in a hospital, a pink or a blue knitted cap often is placed on the baby's head to indicate its sex. The tremendous power of the drive to place newborns into gender categories can be seen in what often is done to trans-sexual babies in America. Instead of allowing the children to grow into adolescence and make decisions themselves about gender identity, the American medical model has generally led in the directions of sexual reassignment surgery (Looy and Bouma, 2005). As soon as a child's sex is known (or assigned), touch behavior takes different forms. Boy and girl babies tend to be touched differently, not only by their parents but by people in general. While boy babies are handled quite matter-of-factly, as if they are tough, caregivers cuddle girl babies, holding them more closely to their bodies and touching them more often and more gently than they do boys (Condry, Condry, and Pogatshnik, 1983). These touches, given by parents and often by siblings both at home and by caretakers outside of the home, socialize children, suggesting to girls that they should expect to be touched often and gently and to boys that they should expect to be "manhandled." Even these very early tactile experiences teach children that appropriate touch is judged as such because of gender considerations.

Within families, not only are boys and girls touched differently, but mothers and fathers relate physically to their babies differently. That difference lays the foundation for the nature of relationships among children and their parents and others. In general, mothers tend to touch babies more than fathers do, even when fathers are highly in-volved in babies' care (Lamb et al., 1982). Mothers' touch tends to ex-press affection and responsiveness while fathers' touch is more playful or instrumental (meaning, fathers touch in order to do things, such as change the child's diaper or carry the child some place) (Popenoe, 1996; Stacey, 1996). However, as is so often the case, these gendered associa-tions are not essentially tied to biology.

Men's and women's touch of babies and infants depends more on their relationship with their children than with their gender. People who feed their babies tend to hold them for a sustained time close to their bodies. Of course, women who breastfeed babies have more physi-cal body contact with them then do women or men who bottle feed babies. Skin-to-skin contact happens naturally during breastfeeding but would seem odd during bottle-feeding. Not only bottle or breastfeed-ing matters, so also does familiarity with babies. Research shows that fathers tend to integrate both nurturing and playful touch more regu-larly with their second (and subsequent) children or with higher birth-weight newborns than with firstborns or premature babies (Goebel, 2002; Shields and Sparling, 1993). When parents routinely care for their children, parental touch repertoires grow, whether those parents are fathers or mothers. This suggests that the gendered polarization of the nature and meaning of touch is highest when parents are superficially engaged in child care and lowest when parents are deeply involved in caregiving.

As children grow into adulthood, they carry with them the sense of how they also should touch others. When men become fathers, the way they touch their own children is heavily influenced by how they themselves had been touched as children (Weiss and Goebel, 2003). In general, according to Pearson, West, and Turner, "women are more likely than men to initiate hugs and touches that express support, affection, and comfort, whereas men more often use touch to direct others, assert power and express sexual interest" (Hall, 1998; Pearson, West, and Turner as quoted in Wood, 2005, p. 137). Very few researchers would argue that the type of touching associated with one or the other gender is the result of essential, biological differences between women and men. Instead, the differences have to do with learned experience and direct teaching both at home and in the context of social and cultural institutions such as day care and school. When, for example, fathers enter into the routine care of their children, especially infants, barriers of touch break down and fathers' touch begins to resemble mothers' in its nurturing qualities, being done for its own sake rather than to accomplish a task.

THE ROLE OF TOUCH IN CHILDHOOD AND ADOLESCENCE

As children grow older, they continue to need touch in their lives. Not just babies but children of all ages benefit from parents' embraces and hugs. This show of physicality reassures children that they are loved. Feeling loved insulates them, at least somewhat, from insecurity, from seeking love from others who may pressure them into sex at an early age, and from susceptibility to the kind of self-hate that leads to eating disorders. When touch is missing in their lives, or when the touch of parents is harmful, children tend to grow up less secure and confident (Solomonica-Levi et al., 2001). Some parents may find it difficult to continue to hold, hug, or sit near a maturing child, perhaps afraid of implicit sexual messages. Nevertheless, there are great goods for the whole family when touch remains an active part of their communal life.

Women who were touched in loving ways as children tend to be less susceptible to eating disorders— a significant benefit of touch for women. Research into women's drive for thinness found that women who were regularly held and touched in a nurturing way as children loved themselves and their bodies more than women who felt themselves deprived of touch as children (Gupta and Schork, 1995). Further, Gia Marson in a research study on college women and eating disorders argues: "a lack of perceived nurturing touch experiences between daughters and mothers during childhood may, in part, add to a young girls' vulnerability for body dissatisfaction as she struggles to accept her body in a society obsessed with the pursuit of unrealistic thinness" (Marson, 2000, p. 5782). As girls grow into women, the ways in which they were touched by their parents remain potent influences. Loving touch meant they were loved, that they were good enough as they were, and they did not have to fit into the mediated mold of thinness in order to earn love. Those early, individual meanings, tend to have the power to trump cultural ones.

Boys, as well as girls, find that touch matters as they grow into adulthood. While research suggests that men's body images are not affected by touch as directly as are women's, their responsiveness to touch and their ability to pass on nurture through touch to others lessens as they grow older. Research on the ways fathers and sons give and receive touch shows that preadolescent boys are held and nurtured more than adolescent boys. The sad irony is that even though adolescent boys and their fathers report that each other's touch matters to them, adolescent boys learn to shy away from their fathers' embraces (Salt, 1991). Research among college-age people shows that in conversational settings, women take the lead in touching; touching others more often than men do and using touch to facilitate conversation (Jones, 1986). When it comes to knowing how to use touch to comfort someone, women are shown to have developed a larger repertoire than men (Dolin & Booth-Butterfield, 1993).

It seems paradoxical, given that care-filled touch is so important to early thriving and subsequent social development, that as boys grow into men, they touch and are touched less and less frequently in a nurturing way. Once they are no longer babies who need to be held to be fed or to have their diapers changed, boys grow more and more physically isolated from those who love them. Why is that, when nurturing touch has been shown to be beneficial to human development? Why would boys and men not seek such touch?

What culturally powerful set of taboos holds them back?

One key answer may have to do with sexuality. As children become adolescents, they start to enter adulthood, where the meanings of touch become even more complicated. That which earlier may have seemed to be just affectionate, now becomes associated with sexuality. Given the prevalence of mediated messages of sexuality that permeate popular culture through the Internet, television, film, and music, it is not surprising that touch of any sort may more easily be given sexual meanings rather than innocently loving ones. Not only the persons involved in affectionate touch but also those watching it impose interpretations on that touch, which is influenced by the symbol systems of mass media as well as the meanings found in the dominant culture. For example, in Northern Hemisphere cultures, much more sexual suspicion crops up in relation to touch than in Southern ones. Out of intentions not to harm one's adolescent child, or not to appear to be too sexual with their children, parents may shy away from hugging and holding their children.

Michel Foucault named this inherent knowledge of how generalized others perceive things the "panopticon." In *Discipline and Punish: The Birth of the Prison* (1977), Foucault suggests that in a prison it does not matter whether any actual person is watching. The sheer understanding of how people in general would view that touch or embrace enforces limits. It does not take an effort of will to recognize the panopticon. Just the opposite holds true. It does not require a prison for the panopticon to operate. By virtue of being socialized into a certain culture, people learn just exactly how different actions will be interpreted by others. For example, it would be the rare Hungarian who would smile indiscriminately in public, knowing the vulnerability it suggests. For many, many years, Hungarians knew that the random observer could turn them in, whether their rulers were the Nazis or the Communists. As a consequence, their interpersonal relationships with neighbors were severely stunted. In like manner, simply by accepting and acting on the limits imposed by the Western panopticon and the limits embedded in that set of cultural meanings on touch, parents, family members, and others truncate the benefits of touch in adolescents' lives.

This analysis, however, does not hold when applied to children who have been sexually abused. When sexual touch from a close adult relative or other adult is part of a child's life, the meanings of touch are always complicated and often haunt a person as he or she grows into adulthood, making them suspicious of any touch and wary of sexuality. Inappropriate expressions of sexuality, forced upon a child, especially by an adult who supposedly loves and has the best interest of the child at heart, do nothing but harm that person. The point here is that when loving intentions and responsive uptakes come together, the effects of touch are beneficial. In the case of sexual abuse, the adult's intentions are not loving but deeply self-serving and twisted, and a child's response is conflicted. He or she knows at some deep level that he or she is being betrayed by someone who claims to love them.

Returning to cases where touch as given and experienced in a child's life is not sexual but loving, at the time of adolescence, even innocently affectionate touches almost inevitably come to be associated with sexuality. In America, this may be particularly and potently taboo for fathers and sons. Same sex touching, especially between boys and men, can take on associations of homosexuality (Floyd & Morman, 2000). These associations provide solid examples of the ways in which context can affect the meaning of actions. In Southern Hemisphere countries, same sex touching is associated with friendship and affection, not necessarily with sexuality. In North America, such is not the case. *Any* touch between fathers and sons may drop dramatically due to those taboo associations. When people, especially fathers, act on these meanings and avoid affectionate touching because they are afraid such touching either will turn boys from heterosexual to homosexual or that such touching indicates that oneself is homosexual, they may perpetuate and even promote an unhealthy sense of self (and deeply mistaken notions of the causes of homosexuality). Touching or avoiding touch because of cultural or personal homophobia communicates volumes about the meaning of touch, meaning that is picked up not only by sons but by anyone who sees fathers and sons relating physically to each other.

Homophobia is not the only source of taboos that might keep parents from hugging and holding their adolescent children. Heterosexual phobias, such as a fear of appearing sexual rather than supportive may also keep parents from touching their growing-up opposite-sex children. As children's bodies develop into adult ones, parent-child relationships change. Parents may be surprised that they experience sexual feelings in relation to their children, and those feelings may make the parents afraid to be as free and easy with their children as they were when the children still looked like children. It is not only parents' fears about their own feelings that may enter in; they may also be afraid of prompting inappropriate sexual responses in their children, and parents, more than children, may be all too aware of the panopticon.

While fears based on incest taboos may serve well in setting reasonable physical boundaries, they may also, paradoxically, cut off the kind of physical contact between parents and children that anchors children's senses of security, thereby hindering the development of healthy self-images, identities, and abilities to make meaningful connections with other people. *Avoiding* touch also sends a strong message—the message that the parent does not love or approve of their child. Thus, dominant cultural meanings of the association of sexuality with touch can discourage life-giving actions between parents and children and harm the capacity of this key human relationship to nurture people.

Not touching children affectionately, even as they enter adolescence, can lead to more emotional damage to children than does touching. Even if adolescents shy away from being hugged, they still want and need it (Salt, 1991). Parental touch is at least one touch between people of unequal social power that can communicate meanings of unconditional love and acceptance, which is something sorely needed by adolescents. When someone feels well and fully loved by parents, it gives that person the inner resources needed to believe oneself a good and loving person and worthy of being treated well by others. Such a feeling of being loved helps people understand what constitutes loving touch, in contrast to abusive touch, and to be able to use that discernment to withstand temptations either to do or to allow bad touch to occur.

It may take a certain sort of bravery to continue to hug, hold, and put an arm around adolescent children and for them to reciprocate. With the onset of puberty, there is an increased awareness on the part of both adults and children of the sexual meanings in touch. Given the fact that mass media present only young and slim people as sexual actors, ones whose bodies appear adolescent, it becomes even more difficult to sort out affection from sex and easier to be suspicious about the meaning of almost any touch.

THE ROLE OF ADULT TOUCH: COMPLICATIONS OF GENDER, SEXUALITY, AND POWER

In adult life, touch continues to play a role in communicating messages about the quality of relationships—about gender, sexuality, and power. American athletes, such as Mark McGwire and Sammy Sosa, engage in elaborate high fives and exuberant full body hugs. Women friends walk arm in arm down the streets of Amsterdam sharing a conversation. A teacher leans over her adult student, placing a hand on his shoulder, guiding the interpretation of a graph. Enemies Yitzhak Rabin and Yasser Arafat warily approach each other, encouraged by President Bill

Clinton, shaking hands in a rare moment of agreement (Clinton, 2004). A mother tenses at the hug of a child from whom she is estranged. Whether knowingly or not, each of these people are saying something about what they feel about the people in their lives. At some level, everyone who observes these interactions constructs opinions about what the touches mean and makes judgments about that meaning.

In adulthood, people play out the deeply coded scripts of their childhood and youth. An unspoken but potent influence on those scripts, a subtext, comes out in how grown-ups touch and are touched. As we saw earlier, adults tend to reenact with their own children the touch they themselves received as children. They tend to revert to autopilot in their daily lives, too. People who *receive* touch, however, tend not to perceive other adults' touches as automatic but rather as meaningful, and at their peril, the inappropriate, unthinking touching behavior of some people continues to offend and harm others because, to return to the point we started with, themes of power and sexuality are central in the meaning of nonverbal communication. Intended or not, those themes make their presence known, as can be seen in cases of domestic violence or sexual harassment.

The point to remember is that humans reap in adulthood what is sown in infancy and childhood. When care is taken with those earliest experiences of touch, particularly by parents, the foundation is laid in children for healthier self-concepts, personal identities, and interpersonal relationships. It is the job of parents to realize their way of touching their children communicates care. Respecting a child's right to appropriate boundaries is up to the parent. Finding ways to help children articulate what they want and need is also up to the parent. Together, children and parents create an ethical, nurturing space for this key form of nonverbal communication, touch.

THREE CASES OF GOOD STRUCTURED PARENTAL TOUCH

Given the good that loving touch for children and families does, it would seem that social and cultural messages that endorse and encourage that sort of physicality would be routine, seen often in news and entertainment media. Such is not the case, however. In this section, analyses of three types of parental touch, "kangaroo care," breastfeeding, and sleeping together in a family bed, shows how something quite benign and indeed, positively helpful, can be portrayed as wrong, even malicious. These three types of touch are discouraged in our day's popular news and entertainment sources. Old-fashioned scripts of power and sexuality fuel the rhetoric of discouragement, driving a wedge between parents and children, rather than helping families communicate and experience care.

The first sort of structured parental touch, laying a baby on one's chest, carries tremendous benefits. Limited research has been done on what is called "kangaroo care," or holding a baby, usually preterm, skin to skin (Anderson, G. C., 1995; Aucott et al., 2002; Engler et al., 2002; Feldman and Eidelman, 2003; Feldman et al., 2002, 2003; Ludington-Hoe, 1993; Tessier, et al., 2003). While the research tends to focus on mothers holding tiny, fragile babies, some studies include fathers. Significantly, the findings are that when parents regularly put babies skin to skin on their chests and hold them there, babies and parents both thrive. It does not seem to matter whether the parent is male or female; bonding takes place and lessens babies' crying and restlessness. Further, not only do parents who practice kangaroo care with their children touch their babies, researchers noticed that the parents touched each other more often and also, as time went on, played with their baby together (Feldman et al., 2002). Through kangaroo care, touch takes on meanings of love and comfort, spilling over from the parents in relation to the child and to the parents in relation to each other.

Breastfeeding would seem to be a logical follow-up to kangaroo care, depending as it does on skin-to-skin contact between mother and child. However, in industrialized Western societies, breastfeeding is anything but a normal practice. Even though it is credited with increasing babies' immunities and contributing to increased health at virtually all stages of life ("Benefits of Breastfeeding," 2008), breastfeeding remains somewhat of a countercultural choice in the Western world. However, in most non-Western cultures, breastfeeding is practiced as the normal way of nurturing a child. When people move to Western cultures from non-Western, researchers suggest that "the rate at which a particular group adopts bottle-feeding and decreases breastfeeding can be used as a measure of the extent to which that culture has replaced its traditional beliefs and practices with those of the western world" (Agnew, Gilmore, and Sullivan, 1997). Recent research shows that most American women (69.5 percent according to "Women's Health USA, 2003") breastfeed their babies in the hospital but, within six months, that percentage slumps to 32.5 percent and within twelve months, to 17 percent (Kam, 2008).

By looking at websites and blogs, we can see many of the social and cultural reasons why women stop breastfeeding, a practice that provides "nature's perfect food" ("Breastfeeding," 2005). Among the reasons, public disapproval ranks highest. According to the American Dietetic Association, 57 percent of Americans disapprove of breastfeeding in public (Kam, 2008). The reason can be seen in this comment by an anti-nursing blogger, who shows a distinctive kind of American prudishness—one that perceives uses of breasts for purposes other than adult heterosexual sexual arousal to be perversely sexual: "By the way, I've always suspected a lot of people who breastfeed their 3 year olds and encourage their kiddies to sleep in bed with them are doing this because of their own attachment issues, not necessarily their kids' benefit" (Walden, 2007). In response, a pro-nursing blogger on milkandhoneydesigns.com posted a comment that highlighted the paradoxes embedded in that attitude, "I find it interesting that breastfeeding beyond infancy is still an issue in our culture. I still nurse my two and a half year old and it causes more of a stir than the latest photo of Britney Spears without underwear. I don't get it. How can we be such a prudish society in one way and not the other. [sic] Breasts don't scare people in our world, seeing them any other way but sexually does" (Walden, 2007).

Given the value of breastfeeding for parents and children, both in terms of nutrition for the baby and development of intimacy and personal security, it would seem logical and reasonable for breastfeeding to be practiced by all but the few who cannot sustain it for physical reasons. It would seem to be an excellent idea to structure leave time from work and to create supportive public space for this practice to become the norm. That has not happened in America. In fact, the opposite is taking place, not due to reasons related to love and care but, instead, to those of sexual taboo in which women who choose to use their breasts for anything but adult heterosexual sexual arousal are off-limits.

It may seem that parents sleeping with babies is but a simple extension of kangaroo care and breastfeeding, on its face a noncontroversial matter of choice for families that would allow parents and children to stay in touch and near each other, with breastfeeding mothers readily available to their babies. If one were to follow this practice of caring touch through popular media sources such as newspapers, however, one would find it portrayed as recklessly endangering children's lives.

Recently, researchers have begun to study "family beds" or "cosleeping," a very old family tradition obscured by the postindustrial, middle-class practice of separating babies from parents. In a family bed, parents and children sleep together. When a baby is very young, this allows the mother to nurse the child with a minimum amount of disturbance. Dr. William Sears, in *Nighttime Parenting* (Sears and White, 1999), argues that not only is breastfeeding enhanced when parents and children share a bed but the babies also benefit from the parents' touch and closeness to them. Dr. James McKenna (1996) argues that cosleeping benefits both parents and children, thus helping women's bodies to tune into babies' needs because of close, regular contact. Other experts find this practice suspect, arguing that the baby may die if a parent should roll over on top of the baby (Task Force on Infant Sleep Position and Sudden Infant Death Syndrome, 2000), or the baby may not develop appropriate independence (Ferber, 1986; Weissbluth, 2005). Families who practice cosleeping are enthusiastic about it. Entire websites, or portions of them, such as The Natural Family Site (www .bygpub.com/natural/family-bed.htm) develop the benefits available to a family that sleeps together.

Given the research on the value of touch in kangaroo care and in early physical development, it would seem that the family bed would be shown as a regular, normal practice. Instead, institutional sources, such as the American Academy of Pediatrics, choose to highlight the potential dangers of parents' sleeping with children, arguing not only that parents might inadvertently smother them but also that some of the deaths attributed to Sudden Infant Death Syndrome (SIDS) may well be from deaths due to cosleeping accidents (Cohen, 1999). In 2002, the U.S. Consumer Product Safety Commission and the Juvenile Products Manufacturers Association warned of dire consequences if babies slept with parents. They presented evidence that during the three-year period from 1999–2001, "at least 180 children under the age of two died after being placed in adult beds" (U.S. Consumer Product Safety Commission, 2002).

What these two sources with financial interests in selling cribs did not add as evidence is that babies die of SIDS, presumably in cribs or other separate beds, at the rate of about three thousand a year ("National Briefing Science and Health," 2001). While any death of a young child is a tragic loss, it is disingenuous, at best, to present crib sleeping as safer than sharing a family bed. One hundred eighty deaths of children in family beds over a three-year period pales in comparison to three thousand *a year* who die in cribs or other beds.

The popular media have picked up on the line of argument offered by the U.S. Consumer Product Safety Commission and the Juvenile Products Manufacturers Association, telling parents in magazines such as *Prevention* that letting babies sleep with them is more dangerous than having babies sleep in cribs (McGinnis, 2004). Other magazines, such as *Newsweek*, attempted to balance their presentation of the warnings about the dangers of family beds with recognition that other experts, such as the American Academy of Pediatrics and the National Institute of Child Health and Human Development, were neutral on the practice (Springen, 2003). However, even as the article attempts to show both sides of the argument, the quotes offer a perspective that highlights dangers, seen from the institutional experts' point of view, rather than the benefits of cosleeping. For example, the *Newsweek* article quotes Marian Willinger from the National Institute of Child Health and Human Development: "If you choose to do this, just be careful" (Springen, 2003) and follows up immediately with a set of caveats: "That means no soft mattresses or water beds, no quilts or duvets, and keep pillows away from the baby. Also, make sure your infant isn't overdressed—it'll get extra warmth from your body, so overheating is a danger. And always remember to put the baby to sleep on its back, not its stomach" (Springen, 2003).

The consequences of mediated representations such as these are chilling. Instead of showing family beds fairly in comparison to separate sleeping, popular media put their thumbs on the scale, tipping the balance in favor of institutional sources. Not coincidentally, these sources are far more likely to advertise in magazines and newspapers than are nonprofit support groups or individual parents.

Not only commercial concerns motivate the rhetoric surrounding popular depictions of family beds. There are gendered symbolic meanings implicit in all the conversation and controversy over family beds, ones that lie deep under the surface of the seemingly simple and very personal choice of a mother and father to share a bed with a baby. The paradox of popular media heightening the dangers of cosleeping, even in the face of strong research findings that promote it, may be explained by looking at the class and gender-based taboos that support the separation of parents and children, especially the nursing couple of mother and baby. Again, two dynamics of nonverbal meaning emerge: power and sexuality.

The first is similar to the way childbirth is framed in America, as shown in the preceding chapter. There, we showed how childbirth no longer is understood as a natural act undergone by women and attended by women. Instead, it is presented as a situation fraught with potential danger, best managed by the "gold standard" of care, defined in America as synonymous with care managed by institutional medical protocols, with surgery as an ever present option (see also Sterk et al., 2002). This notion, of technologically managing what is at base a natural activity, of separating bodies, touch, and care, grows from a worldview that is associated with hegemonic Western masculinity. Class is implicated here, as well as masculine control over women's life events, through placing authority in the hospital and doctors, both of which require significant financial resources for easy access. Significant social pressure exists to move women out of their homes and into hospitals equipped with surgical suites and birthing technology.

In that view, buttressed by hundreds of years of scholarship in science, philosophy, and religion (see *The Less Noble Sex: Scientific, Religious, and Philosophical Conceptions of Woman's Nature* by Nancy Tuana for further development of this claim), women are defined as belonging to the realm of nature and the body, while men are associated with the realm of reason and the mind. In the realm of nature, people supposedly respond to situations based on emotion and instinct instead of rationality. With its assumption of the values of rationality based on the deep tradition of modernism, this point of view can be seen in arguments that suggest it is better for babies to sleep apart from their parents, even in the light of evidence that shows many benefits to parents and children of cosleeping, as well as the linkage of crib sleeping with more deaths than those associated with a family bed. The irony, of course, is that practices framed as rational—engaging in parenting actions that physically separate the bodies of parents and children—do not produce desired results. Well-adjusted children result from parenting practices that are high in touch and high in physical comfort. The evidence shows that modernist assumptions lead to creation of meanings that ultimately do not serve the child or the family, so what is presented as rational actually is not rational at all. It is not coincidental that modernist assumptions line up with industrial-era, class-based practices of middle- to upper-class people sleeping in a separate room from their children.

On an even deeper, perhaps more inaccessible level, operating at the level of taboo, there may be further reasons why there are so few positive presentations of the family bed in popular mediated discourses, and the ones that are there are presented as oddly exotic, bizarre, and dangerous rather than in line with traditional family practices over time and across cultures. In television and film, "bed" serves as a metaphor for sex, not for nightly rest. When a man and woman go to bed or sleep together on television or in film, they are assumed *not to* be sleeping. If a baby is in the bed, that baby disrupts the dominant sexually charged meanings of *bed* and *sleep*. When a baby is present, so also is a strong inhibitor to sexual activity. In American culture, the sexualized meanings given to *bed* and *sleep* trump their functional meanings. As a result, media images contribute to the assumption that a husband's prerogative to easy, regular, sexual activity with his wife should outweigh the temporary needs of a baby for its mother's nursing and parental closeness and touch.

As the nursing baby grows into a weaned toddler, her or his need for the nurture found in a family bed lessens. So, naturally and incrementally, cosleeping usually transforms into separate sleeping, usually at a pace that the child determines, thereby allowing the child's increasing maturity to enter into decision-making. Discourses that intervene and disrupt the family bed in the name of children's independence or parents' sexual privacy are only meaningful in a context where separation, independence, and an understanding that any touch is necessarily sexual are normalized. That point of view, resonating profoundly with Victorian-era mores and modernist life assumptions, is highly gendered because of the male-oriented heterosexual assumptions that so deeply animate it. A family bed more obviously serves the nursing couple of mother and baby than the sexual couple of wife and husband and, as such, may go against the grain of the meaning of *bed* as popularly mediated in America.

All of these topics of structured family touch, kangaroo care, breastfeeding, and sharing a family bed provide ways for families to use good touch at the earliest of ages. As the research on touch shows, loving touch creates bonds among parents and children, helps children feel securely attached, reduces gender polarization in the ways mothers and fathers hold and touch babies, and sets up children for healthier adolescence and adulthood. Through creating ways to be together physically, families are able to tap into all those very good relationally based outcomes.

REFLECTIONS

Touch, one of the first senses to develop, is able to metacommunicate loving, responsiveness, caring support, appropriate control, and the opposites of each. Done well, it allows babies and grown people to thrive, allows the family system to make mutual decisions about care. So often, the meaning remains unsaid, which forces people to fill in gaps; to intuit meaning. Given all this, it makes such good sense to shape life with language as well as nonverbal communication and with full consciousness of the value of good touch. Cultural messages about how parents and children should relate physically are charged with sexual and power subtexts. It takes real human bravery to determine to do what's right for children—to hold them close, to have parents share both instrumental and nurturing touch with babies, and to ignore social and cultural taboos in order to raise healthy children.

In sum, the literature on the practices and meanings related to babies, adults, and touch strongly supports regular, loving physical contact. The more routinely adults touch babies, not only to do a task, such as change a diaper, but also just to snuggle, whether skin to skin or in a shared bed, the less touch carries polarized gendered meanings. When adults are physically in touch with babies, babies thrive and adults and babies bond more securely together. Starting life this way may be personal, private, and located within families; the good initiated there can move out into public life. Through developing strong senses of security as children, adults can pass on that roundedness to others, not only within families but also within society and culture through the work adults do as researchers, teachers, caregivers, media producers, reporters, bloggers, and so on. Meanings of good touch must be promoted, not just received as inevitably tainted with messages of power and sexuality. In so doing, the paradoxes involved in touching can be resolved and the taboos faced squarely and honestly. When this happens, people are practicing an ethic of care.

3

BODIES IN MOTION

Paradoxes and Taboos of
Men's Sport

In virtually every country around the world, men's soccer is the su-
preme sport. In the Netherlands, one of the charter members of the
worldwide soccer federation called the Federation Internationale de
Football Association (FIFA), there are more than one million Dutch
boys and men and more than one hundred thousand Dutch girls and
women who play soccer (KNVB, 2007). In fact, men make up 91 percent
of the Dutch soccer players. Not only is soccer the most popular sport
to play, it is also the premier Dutch spectator sport (KNVB, 2007). Five
of the top-ten most-watched television programs in 2007 were men's
soccer games (SKO, 2007).

Maleness goes together in Dutch soccer with national pride and
identity. When the Dutch men's national team participates in European
or World Cup games, orange flags fly in the deserted streets, while
the pubs and taverns are filled with cheering spectators. In contrast,
women's soccer rarely appears on television. The Dutch generally
assume that because of its physical demands Dutch soccer simply is
more suitable for males than for females (Knoppers & Anthonissen,
2004; Knoppers & Elling, 2001); a subtle taboo remains in place in the
Netherlands against women's playing soccer competitively and at the
highest levels.[1]

In contrast, men's soccer is not the most popular spectator sport in
the United States. Instead, it is framed mainly as a participatory sport
for both females and males. Youth participants far outnumber adults.
Further, soccer rarely is associated with American national identity,
instead, sports such as men's football, basketball, and baseball (the lat-

ter is known as "the national pastime") line up far more closely with identity. Perhaps as a consequence of there being no gender taboo against women who play soccer, a unique aspect of American soccer is that it is associated with women as well as men and played by about equal numbers (Longman, 2001). The U.S. women's national team has won the World Cup twice, as well as the gold medal in the Athens and Beijing Olympics. It continues to be highly ranked internationally. Attendance and interest in women's soccer at the 1999 World Cup competition broke all records for a women's sport. Ninety thousand people attended the final, which was held in the Rose Bowl; forty million Americans watched it on television (Longman, 2001). Yet, the paradox is that even such success and interest was initially not enough to sustain professional women's soccer. After just two years of operation, its league folded in 2003, although women's professional soccer later made a comeback (Porteus, 2006).

Sport is a key site of gendered physicality. As such, along with birthing and touch, it is a fitting place for analysis of the paradoxes and taboos of gendered meanings. Ever since the Greeks, sport has been framed culturally as a place where competitiveness and physical domination, long the domain of masculinity, receive all the attention. All sport-related concerns, such as participation, leadership, management, governance, and media coverage once were the domain of men. This social fact about male dominance is connected to meanings given to sport and to participants' bodies. These meanings are multilayered, complex, contradictory, and always changing, especially given women's participation in sport. Their participation has increased dramatically in the past 150 years. Even though men comprise two-thirds of elite sport athletes in organized sports, there are no longer any sports where women do not compete. Assumptions about the appropriateness of women's participation in sport have shifted. More than 150 years ago, competitive physicality and middle-class femininity were seen as antithetical. Now, the two are perceived to be more congruent.

Given women's increasing participation and acceptance in sport, it is tempting to argue that it is only a matter of time before their presence and power is on a par with men's. If an ethic of care animated decision-making at all personal and institutional levels of sport, women and men would share its playing space, both literally and symbolically. We are not yet at that point. Underlying social and cultural forces still allow men to use sport as a place where they can distance themselves from things associated with women. This chapter will analyze possible reasons why deeply rooted gender prejudices, based on values of control and gender polarity rather than care and gender equity, continue to structure sport participation, spectatorship, governance, and leadership. It will explore how men may use sport to differentiate themselves from all that is womanly and how meanings given to sport participation continue to change and strengthen meanings given to gender. Due to the increasing importance and role that sport plays in the gendering of physicality, the differences in the historical processes through which men's and women's sport have evolved, and the unique formal structuring of sport into men's and women's sport, we devote two chapters to this topic.

SPORTING MASCULINITIES

Over time, the meanings that we give to sport and gender interact with each other and evolve, but men's sport continues to be a site where men can differentiate and distance themselves from what is seen as womanly.

Up until the middle of the nineteenth century, sport was not routinely included as part of either men's or women's education. The curricula at elite boys' schools in England at that time included sport because of the confluence of several societal factors (Giulianotti, 1999; Hargreaves, 1994; Messner & Sabo, 1994; Putney, 2001), including work, health, war, and sexuality. The shift from a largely agrarian society to an industrialized multiclass society meant there was less need for male physical work. In addition, developments in the area of medicine equated fresh air and exercise with health. The omnipresent threat of war provided a third factor that strengthened the discourse about boys' participation in sport. After all, wars required strong masculine bodies and leaders. A fourth concern was the worry that both society and Protestantism were becoming increasingly feminized. A fifth factor increased the perceived need to incorporate sport programs in curricula of elite schools for boys—the worry that the seclusion of these schools from the rest of society and their all-male environment might tempt boys to engage in the vices of masturbation and homosexuality. It was assumed that through their participation in sport boys would be safe from both of these vices, turning their thinking and actions instead toward manliness, which was equated with heterosexuality. At that time (1880s), homosexuality was defined as being the opposite of manliness. The values assigned to sport, heterosexuality, and manliness began to overlap and gradually became congruent (Townson, 1997).

Although its history with sport is complex, an important Western cultural institution, Protestant Christianity, lined itself up with secular culture in seeing sport as a way to stave off the perceived creeping feminization of culture. Up until the middle of the nineteenth century, many Protestants condemned sport for adult men because participating and watching took time that better could be spent on personal faith development and on constraining the body and its urges (Putney, 2001). Instead of going to church on Sunday, more and more men were going to saloons, to lodges, and later (after 1888) to golf courses. It was not long before women made up the majority of churchgoers and volunteers in social organizations. Even religious symbols and words in hymns ("Gentle Jesus Meek and Mild") were seen as feminine. Christians, especially Protestants, made a concerted effort to find a way to reinvigorate men's lives with robust masculine values.

Consequently, people of all sorts gradually began to see sport as the ideal place where boys and young men could learn to control their tempers, desires, and affections—learning what it means to be gentlemen and leaders. Religiously inflected virtues of morality and manliness learned in sport were assumed to be transferable to all realms of adult life (Ladd & Matthisen, 1999; Miracle & Rees, 1994). For example, soccer participation was assumed to "make scared and pale boys into sturdy and self confident men" (KNVB, 1997, p. 8). Participation in sport was seen as a way to invigorate young men and to prevent them from becoming effeminate. Through their participation in sport, they could differentiate themselves from what was associated with all womanly things at that time (Putney, 2001). Being real men, therefore, meant showing a masculinity that was associated with heterosexuality, leadership, and Protestant Christian values (Cahn, 1994; Hargreaves, 1994). The overlap of meanings given to Christianity, sport, a heroic style of masculinity, and heterosexuality came to be seen as common sense or self-evident because all were associated with God's intentions for the natural male body

This nineteenth-century discourse about sport has been called "muscular Christianity." It framed Jesus as a manly man who engaged in a male trade (carpentry), was tough (survived forty days in the desert), and was aggressive (he overturned the moneychangers' tables). Muscular Christianity was supported by an ideology that assumed that a physically healthy body strengthens spirituality and pleases God and that sport participation teaches moral values (Putney, 2001). The founding of the Young Men's Christian Association (YMCA) in 1844 in England was explicitly based on this ideology. The YMCA initially was created as a place where working-class urban boys and men could develop these virtues. Later, the YMCA moved on to college campuses and moved away from its working-class roots to become a movement where middle-class men could enhance their Christian character through the development of physical prowess (Brief history, n.d.).

Muscular Christianity and the YMCA grew on both sides of the Atlantic. In the United States, Springfield College trained leaders for the YMCA. James Naismith, the creator of basketball and a faculty member at Springfield, invented basketball as a sport intended to stimulate men's moral and physical growth. In Europe, the discourse of muscular Christianity was a basis for the development of sport clubs along religious lines (in addition to criteria based on social class). Thus, the creation of Protestant clubs, Catholic clubs, working-class clubs, and so on played a significant role in the development of modern sport. In many ways, sport contributed to religiosity and vice versa.

Gradually however, the connection of sport to religiosity lost its power as key leaders in the movement of muscular Christianity died, as secularization continued to be a societal force, and as Western sport moved away from Christian roots and became professionalized. The *C* in YMCA was de-emphasized but not the *M* (Schippert, 2003).

However, it is not difficult to find remnants of the ideology of muscular Christianity embedded in discourses about sport today. American schools often base their arguments for the inclusion of athletic programs on the moral and leadership skills that sport participation purportedly teaches. Similarly, many American churches and Catholic and Protestant high schools and colleges sponsor sport teams in order to boost enrollment or increase membership; to offer a holistic education or program; to enhance their public-relations profile; and to train leaders for physical education, sport, recreation, wellness, and sport ministries (Ladd & Matthisen, 1999). Programs such as Athletes in Action and places such as the Lord's Gym also continue to combine the meanings given to religion and to sport. In 1979, the late Pope John Paul II advocated muscular Christianity through sport participation and created an office for the church and sport (Watson, Weir, & Friend, 2005). In December 2006, Cardinal Tarcisio Bertone, the secretary of state of the Vatican, considered having the Vatican field its own soccer team to compete at the elite level (Vatican, 2006; UPI, 2006).[2] Billy Graham regularly used sport stars in his crusades. Religious fundamentalists engaged not only in evangelism for athletes, tourists, and spectators, but have also used major sport events as sites for terrorist acts (Watson, Weir, & Friend, 2005).

In general, there seems to be little difference between religious and nonreligious institutions in their discursive practices in and about sport, even though one might expect to see more care-based rhetoric coming from religious institutions. As Ladd and Matthisen (1999) argue, the symbol system and discourse of sport ministries rely disproportionately on the culture of sport and athletics, not on discourse and teaching drawn primarily from the Bible and theology. Although the associations between sport and religiosity have changed in the past 150 years, the discourse of sport has stayed true to its association with a desirable masculinity. In fact, those connections continue to be strengthened through an increase in societal emphasis on men's professional sports, as mediated by the Web, newspapers, and television.

Burstyn (1999) and Messner (1992, 2002) have pointed out that currently more men than ever before attend, read, watch, and talk about (men's) sport and have increasingly more opportunities to do so. Messner (1988) has argued that the supposed decrease in the importance of male athleticism and physicality in many areas of society and the seeming increase of women participants in all areas of life (including sport) has strengthened the importance of sport for men. Burstyn has noted that:

the ties that have bound athletes to their communities—whether in working-class England or postcolonial Africa—are being unraveled by commercialization and free trade in athletic labor. As the ties of locality, ethnicity, and nation come more and more undone, the ties of gender, of masculinity, become increasingly important. (p. 25)

Sport still provides an arena where men can prove they are real men, that is, heterosexual and superior to women. In a pithy aphorism, Nelson (1994) argues that "the stronger women get, the more men love football." Televised events such as Monday Night Football, the World Series, or NBA matches offer boys and men (regardless of race and social class) many opportunities to identify with and to construct the idea of men as being physically superior to women. Because some men are faster than all women, the assumption and privileges of physical superiority logically seem to be extended to all men, fallacy though that may be (Messner, 1988, 2002). Therefore, many men may look to sport to differentiate themselves from what is associated with women and womanly, and the culture of sport supports them in that activity.

Even though they may be unable to perform at a professional level, many men find that sport provides them with the images and/or models of athletic masculinities they can share as a meaningful fantasy of masculinity. In his study about the importance of football to American men, Messner (1990) finds that one reason ex-athletes identify with sport and with male athletes is that the heroic acts of the latter prove that men can do physical things, such as tackling, in ways that women cannot. So ingrained is the supposed superiority of men over women that many of the men involved in Messner's study were oblivious to the fact that they themselves were incapable of doing what professional football players do. Media depictions of men's sport construct the vision of all able-bodied men as physically similar, whether or not they are young, strong, or talented.

Sexuality

As we pointed out earlier, one key motivator underlying the organization of modern sport was to keep boys from engaging in homosexuality and, instead, to strengthen their identification with and commitment to heterosexuality. The symbolic connection between heterosexuality and sport participation continues today and seems to be so self-evident that the sexual identity of men and boys who do not identify with sports such as soccer (outside of the United States), football, basketball, or hockey may be questioned.

Meanings given to male physicality vary by sport, however, and are used to differentiate among men as well as to marginalize entire groups of men. Consider, for example, the markedly different meanings of masculinity given to figure skating and football. It is clear that not all sports sustain dominant discourses about masculinities—only those that have traditionally been associated with qualities believed to mark heterosexual men and that emphasize strength, the giving and taking of pain, record-setting performances and mental toughness, support for male bonding and affection, and a discouragement of behaviors associated with femininities or gay masculinities (Connell, 2005; Messner, 1992). Giving and taking pain and engaging in violent and aggressive behavior are often associated with male heterosexuality. This is a far cry from the gentlemanly behaviors of Christian athletes who participated in muscular Christianity 150 years ago (Burstyn, 1999). Currently, men and boys who care little about sport or who throw or play poorly are told that they act "like girls" and may be labeled as effeminate (Messner, 1990, 2002; Pronger, 1990), thereby marginalizing women and gay men, ignoring or ridiculing the multiplicity of ways they enact and participate in sport. Men who walk away from aggressiveness or are deemed not to be aggressive enough, are often called fags or wimps. There are many stories about the physical and emotional pain men have endured as boys, or that boys encounter now, because of their ineptness in sport skills (see for example, Parker, 1996; Pascoe, 2003; Swain, 2000).

Sport, therefore, has become a site of gender struggle where men and boys are expected to show behaviors that distinguish them from women and from gay men. Although sport itself may be associated with heterosexuality, male athletes still must prove (on and off the field) that they are not womanly. This pressure often leads men to demean women and gay men. It is not surprising, then, that the incidence of violent and sexual assault against women is relatively higher among male athletes than nonathletes (Crossett, Benedict, & McDonald, 1995; Curry, 1998). This strong emphasis on demonstrating a tough heterosexuality in men's sport has another dimension to it as well—the cooption and subversion of the appearance of homosexuality. Many team sports allow male athletes to be physically affectionate with each other in the sport setting in ways that are associated with gay men outside of sport, such as fanny slapping, chest bumps, hugging, and, showering together. At the same time, the meanings assigned to actions often associated with homosexuals have to be subverted, so that a safe heterosexuality remains firmly in place. One way this is enforced is that openly gay men are rarely welcome in men's (team) sports (Anderson, E., 2000; Pronger, 1990). It is not surprising, then, that very few football and basketball players have come out as being gay, only doing so after they end their sport careers (Kopay, 1977; Anderson, E., 2000).

One professional basketball player who came out (after retiring) is John Amaechi. Sheridan (2007), a writer for ESPN who reviewed the book Amaechi wrote about his experiences in the NBA, describes the contradictions in the ways sexuality is performed in this context. Rather than rant about his teammates, Amaechi points out the locker room's sexual ironies. "They checked out each other's cocks. They primped in front of the mirror. . . . They tried on each other's $10,000 suits and shoes. . . . And I'm the gay one. Hah!" While penis sizes were being checked out, Amaechi says, he "stood in the corner in baggy clothes or wrapped in an oversized towel." That scene—Amaechi, standing alone, as his heterosexual teammates engage in homosocial behavior—is the book's lasting ironic image.

Thus, meanings given to sport often celebrate and privilege a certain macho type of heterosexual masculinity and denigrate anything that is associated with homosexual masculinities although that behavior can be quite contradictory.

Race

The symbolic privileges that accrue to athletes do not extend uniformly to all heterosexual men, however, but vary by other social relations such as race and class. Because everyone has a chance to win, sport is assumed to be a place of equal opportunity. After all, success does not depend on one's skin color or ethnic background, but on the final score. Even though sport is often seen as being color blind, it is not (Lapchick, 2006). Elite black athletes are found in a relatively small number of sports. Black athletes have to be better than white athletes to be selected so that mediocrity seems to be a white luxury. Further, the percentage of black coaches and managers is significantly less than the percentage of black athletes. In addition, the disproportionate participation rates of black athletes in certain sports have played a significant role in framing the dominant discourses about race both inside and outside of sport.[3]

Black and white men are often represented differently by the media and in sport discourses.[4] Assumptions about black and white physicalities influence virtually everything having to do with sport, including who is chosen as broadcasting reporters and anchors, as athletes, which sport to broadcast, how large various people's salaries should be, what position should be assigned, who should coach and manage teams, and so forth.[5] Racialized discourses acknowledge the achievements of black men but often attribute their excellence to physical superiority in strength and explosive power, rather than to mental abilities. The upshot is that black athletes tend to be portrayed as athletes for whom sport comes naturally, while white athletes are assumed to have worked hard to develop their athletic talents. These racialized assumptions have not been proven (Hall, R. E., 2001; Harrison, 1998; Harrison & Lawrence, 2004). Instead, research shows that there is no evidence that black and white nonathletes differ in capacity to learn and excel in sport skills, so it cannot be maintained that race matters in relation to an ability to master sports (Coakley, 2007; Davis & Harris, 1998). Further, as Coakley has pointed out, assuming the natural physical superiority of blacks relies on nothing but flawed race logic. White Canadians may excel in ice hockey and Norwegians in team handball, but their success has seldom been attributed to their natural abilities as white athletes.

In addition, although black male athletes may be revered because of their accomplishments, their power and ability to make things happen in sport off the field often are reduced to stereotypes. Disch and Kane (2000) explain how this happens.

> To be an exemplar of masculinity puts the black male athlete in an ambiguous position with respect to race by affording him an experience that, in this racist society, is unique: he will be seen first as a man and second as a black man. This privileged status that the black male athlete enjoys against other black men does not erase his racial identity, however. Sport works paradoxically to forge solidarity in that while it unites men around an anachronistic ideal of masculinity, it also manages to differentiate them by race and class. (p. 115)

These often-ignored differences in symbolic privileges that accrue to white and to black athletes intersect with social class as well.

Social Class

Although race may seem to be more visible in sport because it is so clearly embodied, less visible social relations such as social class play a role in the ways in which we give meanings to sport. Many boys and men, regardless of their athletic status and race, have benefited materially and discursively from the celebration of athletic masculinities, through receiving scholarships, coaching, jobs, and status and fame. Thus, it may seem that sport is class-blind and that success depends solely on talent. That just is not the case.

Meanings assigned to sport participation and opportunities often vary by the social class of the participants (Mehus, 2005; Scheerder,

Vanreusel, & Taks, 2005; Stempel, 2005; Wilson, 2002). For example, many Olympic sports that originated in the Western world tend to be rooted in the lifestyles of the middle to upper class, such as fencing, rowing, skiing, and equestrian events. The emphasis in discourses about sports associated with the upper middle-class people is more on intelligent leadership and strategic play than on physical intimidation and strength. In contrast, bravado and risk-taking tend to receive more attention in sports associated with the working class (Laberge & Albert, 1999), although this is also changing as we show further on in the discussion about extreme sports.

Regardless of social class, however, all sports can be used as a place where working-, middle-, and upper-class males can emphasize ways in which they differ from women and gay men, which could be thought of as a preferred style of masculinity. The characteristics associated with white, middle-class, athletic masculinities tend to color all other constructions of masculinity in identity work.[6] For instance, male non-athletes interviewed by Davison (2000) about their physical-education experiences as boys, were very aware that if they did not want to be marginalized, they had to show a preferred type of athletic masculinity through physical gestures, size, and stature. Pascoe (2003), in an exploration of how boys understood and negotiated masculinities, found that boys used the male athlete or jock as a reference point in their own identities. Boys who were or had been top athletes in dominant boys' sports were allowed to be active in activities with low masculine status, such as drama, without losing their jock status because they had a history of athleticism. Boys who lacked that close association with dominant sports still connected up with a jock image by showing interest in such sports, past athletic history, and having athletic friends. Renold (2004), who also looked at the ways boys associate themselves with athletic masculinities, argues that boys who had no interest in sports disparaged girls and femininities more so than did the athletic/popular boys. In other words, boys who cannot connect to athletic masculinities may try to identify with a masculinity that strongly disparages girls and womanly or girly behaviors. Obviously, then, meanings given to men's sport still play a significant role in the gender identity of young men and boys.

Meanings given to social relations in sport, including social class, are, however, constantly being negotiated, both in Europe and in North America. At first, soccer was played by upper-class men in the Netherlands and became associated with them. Gradually, it became a sport played by the working class, as well. They organized their own sport teams and clubs as upper-class men moved on to other sports such as tennis and field hockey. Through their participation in and eventual domination of soccer, working-class men challenged the idea that soccer belonged to the upper class. In the United States, soccer became a class-based sport as well. It was primarily constructed as a middle- to upper-class sport in the 1990s; the now defunct North American Soccer League started youth programs for boys and girls in suburbs as part of its efforts to promote an interest in soccer in the United States (Andrews, 1999; Henry & Comeaux, 1999). Because of its suburban location, youth soccer was and is primarily played by boys and girls from suburban, white, middle-class families, hence the politically powerful category of 'soccer mom,' so often referenced in 1990s presidential races. Soon, soccer in the United States became symbolically positioned as the opposite of the more aggressive, more socially mixed men's team sports of football, basketball, and hockey. Soccer was assumed to be based on strategy and intelligence as well as skill, rather than on muscle power and physical intimidation. As we pointed out earlier, these meanings assigned to sport tend to be class based. Consequently, the meanings connecting masculinities with certain sports are contextual and can change over time.

CHALLENGING SOCIAL RELATIONS THROUGH AND IN SPORT

Challenges and shifts in the meaning of sport occur. Two areas where social relations could affect, and be affected by, sport include extreme sports and religious use of sport and sport images. Analysis shows, however, that both inevitably get pulled back toward hegemonic race and class-based meanings. This backward movement makes it difficult to include women and gay men in definitions, practices, and discourses about sport, moves which are necessary if sport is to become a place that displays an ethic of care, rather than control.

Extreme Sports

In extreme sports, such as skateboarding, snowboarding, BMX biking, windsurfing, and street luge, all individual rather than team sports, traditional sport meanings appear to be challenged every day. While traditional sports were formally organized for upper-class young men to combat the perceived feminization and secularization of society, extreme sports were created by participants themselves as a reaction to dominant class and gender-based practices in mainstream sport.[7] Ironically, the majority of these rebellious athletes resemble those who participate in traditional sports, that is, they tend to be male and come from white middle- to upper-class backgrounds (Beal, 1996; SGMA, 2004; Wheaton, 2004). A closer look at the development of snowboarding shows the complexity and fluidity of discursive practices that connect masculinities and sport.

Snowboarding evolved out of a growing male discontent with those formal and informal rules and practices unique to traditional ski culture, such as proper clothing and behavior before, during, and after skiing. Snowboarding, like other action sports, began as a highly individualized activity in which participants set their own rules and created their own skill set and culture. In snowboarding, as in all action sports, the emphasis lies on authenticity, that is, creativity and expression of the true self through the development of a unique personal style (Anderson, K., 1999; Beal, 1996; Wheaton, 2004). At first, relatively few formal and informal rules structured these sports; snowboarding practices exemplified resistance to dominant sport cultures. Their rebellion initially cost snow boarders a welcome at ski resorts. However, as the popularity of snowboarding continued to grow, resistance lessened, so that by 2003 about one-third of all those on the ski slopes were snowboarders (SGMA, 2004).

Rebellious though they may be against traditional ski rules and norms, snowboarders themselves engage in gendered practices. Even though part of the appeal of snowboarding and other extreme sports was their repudiation of mainstream sport masculinities, gender differentiation, especially masculinity marking, soon became part of extreme sports, as well. Fewer than a third of the snowboarders, skaters, BMX riders, and wind surfers are girls and women. Consequently, as in mainstream sports, boys often practice extreme sports in all-male environments. Girls are only allowed in when they perform exceptionally well; then their femininity is coopted as they are alluded to as one of the boys (Beal, 1996; Van der Schaaf, 2005, 2007; Wheaton, 2004).

Symbolic differentiation from women and all that is associated with women is part and parcel of extreme sports. Dominant masculinities in snowboarding and other extreme sports are based on images of street youth (boys) and gangsters. Websites and Zines carry names such as Doctor Danger, Play Hard, Extremist, Concussion Magazine, and Adrenalin Playground. They portray images associated with aggressive and fearless boys. Male athletes explain the relative lack of females in their sport by stating that girls are not fearless or aggressive enough to participate and often lack the necessary strength to perform well (Beal, 1996; Karsten & Pel, 2000; Van der Schaaf, 2005, 2007). Inept athletes are called fags, gays, or girls. In other words, participants in extreme sports may create new forms of masculinity, but they also use control-based gender and sexuality discourses reminiscent of those pervasive in many mainstream or traditional sports (Anderson, K., 1999).

Because of the rough-edged masculinity, youth, and social class of its participants, snowboarding became attractive to Olympic and commercial interests. In 1996, it became an official Olympic sport. Ironically, although snowboarding began as a way for teenage boys to rebel against existing class and gender structures, when snowboarding became an Olympic sport, its resistance aspect was blunted through commodification and commercialization. Yet, like most action sports, snowboarding was and continues to be marketed as a sport of youthful resistance. Numbers of participants alone do not bring in sponsors. It seems "[t]he stylistic resistance of the [snowboarding] subculture is what makes it valuable to the advertiser" (Heino, 2000, p. 184). Even though more men play badminton and table tennis than snowboard, the media pay significantly more attention to snowboarding (SMGA, 2004). When advertisers and commercial sponsors want to attract a young male audience, they feature outstanding snowboarders and (male) athletes in other extreme sports. A style of masculinity that incorporates youthful resistance is attractive and sells well, and, as it sells, it becomes mainstream. Thus, the commodification of extreme sports tends to mute their rebellious aspects, making them acceptable as white, middle- to upper-class sports for boys and men.

The world of extreme sports, therefore, is filled with contradictions and complexity. Extreme sports are places where participants can rebel against class- and gender-based behaviors and traditions in other sports, forming what they see as authentic masculinities.[8] Yet, they also use these extreme sports to differentiate themselves from that which they connect with as womanly. Therefore, both resistance and complicity coexist in these relatively new forms of sport. In part, the resistance to

traditional sport masculinities may also mark resistance to the participation of women in many of those sports. Possibly the participation of
many women in sports such as basketball, hockey, and tennis means
that such sports may not always serve as a place for many males to differentiate themselves from that which they define as womanly.

Muscular Christianity

A meaning-filled subset of mainstream culture, religion, offers a micro-
cosmic view of a potential arena of resistance to the controlling rhetoric
of sport that excludes women and gay men. After all, churches often offer space, as does sport, where men may engage in behaviors associated
with femininity and are allowed to be emotionally intimate with other
men without being denigrated or seen as feminized. This permission is
sometimes linked to physicality. The nineteenth-century phenomenon
of muscular Christianity comprised one such space. Contemporary ones
include the organizational practices of the evangelical men's support
group, Promise Keepers (Beal, 1996).

The creation of Promise Keepers and its attendant discursive forms
were in part an attempt to reconcile dominant discourses about masculinity with several elements common to the lives of evangelical
men, such as emotions, concern for domesticity, and religiosity—all
qualities traditionally associated with femininities. This permission is
given, however, in a context where the institutional church and sport
intersect, both arenas that are associated with celebrated forms of
masculinity, thereby keeping it a safe space for men to express spiri-
tual yearning and emotionality without seeming to compromise their
manliness. The Promise Keepers movement has tended to address the
collective fear of men of being seen as womanly by equating manliness
with godliness. Men who are Promise Keepers develop strong homo-
social bonds and emotional expressiveness with each other, emphasize
being godly, not gay, and use sport arenas and settings for large con-
ferences where physical contact is possible. Such events are somewhat
reminiscent of the post-touchdown pile-on of male athletes evidenced
during professional football games in the United States (Bartkowski,
2000). The male homosociality of Promise Keepers, as with the exclu-
sive maleness of many churches' and denominations' clergy, is often
described in terms of family ties and brotherly love and thus avoids
associations with homosexuality.

Thus, instead of urging men to celebrate femininities and to counter the devaluation of them and thereby practice an ethic of care that includes all humans within it, Promise Keepers creates an oddly polarized masculinity that incorporates aspects of behaviors usually associated with women, while simultaneously employing meanings associated with valued masculinities in order to differentiate themselves from women. As long as this differentiation is deemed necessary, sport itself will evolve in order to support such differentiation (cf. Messner, 1988), and religious movements can draw on and reinforce those meanings.

These two examples show how even seemingly revolutionary uses and associations of sport find themselves pulled back into dominant meanings of gender control and polarity. Extreme sports' differentiation from mainstream sports on grounds of age and class diminishes over time. Evangelical men's movement appropriation of sport fails to distinguish sports' meaning from mainstream sports' meaning and imports into Protestant Christianity a certain type of masculine hegemony, rather than transforming sport by Christian ideas and ideals. It is ironic that a context uniquely equipped to practice and promote care, religion based on equality before God, fails to find a way to draw that value into one of its social practices.

CONCLUSION

Men's physical and discursive practices of sport, therefore, are not neutral activities but meaningfully intersect with gender, social class, race, and sexuality. Sport continues to be an arena where a celebrated masculinity can be created, one that depends on differentiating itself from certain types of femininities and from homosexuality.

These masculine meanings change continually. Boys and young men rebel against dominant masculinity forms and create alternative sports, such as snowboarding, where they can construct other masculinities. Ironically, the gender system being what it is, these masculinities tend to rely on gender and sexual differentiations as well. Obviously, then, meanings given to sport continually shift and new sports will continue to be created as long as sport is an arena where gender differentiation continues to play a role. We will know, as a culture, that real change in the direction of an ethic of care has happened when women and men all are invited onto the playing field, bringing their selves and their ways of being and doing along with them.

History shows that as social and cultural importance attached to men's sport increases, so also a need increases to circumscribe women's participation. Gender differentiation remains perceived as crucial. As women's participation in mainstream sport has increased, those who feel a need to distinguish between that which is perceived as manly from womanly may well create and continue to develop sport forms designed to exclude women. Therefore, their history in sport is quite different from men's as we shall see in the following chapter.

NOTES

1. A new division of sponsored women's teams began play in 2007–2008.

2. The next day he said he was only joking and that he was too busy to organize such a team (UPI, 2006).

3. In the United States, black male athletes tend to be relatively overrepresented in several sports such as basketball, athletics, boxing, and football and relatively underrepresented in other sports (golf, rugby, swimming, and wrestling). About 12 percent of the American population is African-American while 80 percent of the players in professional basketball, 67 percent in football and 18 percent in baseball are African- American (Coakley, 2007). Although Dutch sport organizations do not collect demographic data about the ethnic and/or racial background of their members, minority athletes seem to be overrepresented in such sports as soccer, combat sports, track and field, baseball, and cricket, and underrepresented in such sports as volleyball, field hockey, tennis, skating, and cycling (Elling, Knoppers & De Knop 2001).

4. See for example Davis & Harris, 1998; Knoppers & Elling, 2001 for a detailed discussion of racial representation in the sport media.

5. For an extended discussion of race and sport, see Davis & Harris, 1998; Lapchick, 2006.

6. See for example Connell, 2000, 2005; Messner, 1992; Pascoe, 2003.

7. See Beal, 1996; Wheaton, 2004 for an in-depth focus on the development, growth, and meanings given to extreme sports.

8. These associations overlap with each other because the jock image is rooted in middle-class norms and values (Pascoe, 2003).

4

BODIES IN MOTION
Women's Sport as Undoing Gender?

Initially organized to combat the perceived feminization and secularization of society, sport participation and femininity appeared to be polar
opposites. About 150 years ago, women's primary role and godly duties
were assumed to be childbearing and caring for children, husband,
and household. Most sports were deemed "naturally" inappropriate for
girls because they did not seem to fit the homebound Victorian ideal
for white, middle- to upper-class women. Sport historian Ellen Gerber
(1974) describes this discourse about women's participation in sport in
the nineteenth century:

> Sport takes one out of the home and into the tempting, defiling world.
> Sport places participants in positions where their flesh is exposed and
> their emotions are expressed; the [Victorian] ideal required modesty,
> propriety, and circumspectness. Furthermore, by exposing the face and
> reproductive organs to possible injury, sport endangers the ultimate Vic-
> torian goal: the twin functions of attracting a man and bearing a child.
> (p. 12)

At that time, medical experts argued that women who were intellectually and/or physically active would have trouble bearing children
because these activities drew energy away from the uterus to other
parts of the body (Cahn, 1994; Hargreaves, 1994). Experts feared that
physically and intellectually active women might bear blue babies, that
is, children who suffer from a lack of oxygen.

Gradually, however, at least for the middle and upper classes, assumptions about women's physicality began to change. Middle- to

upper-class women had always participated in leisure and recreational sports such as tennis, horseback riding, and golf. Little by little, the health and moral discourses about sport participation began to apply to women as well as to men and women entered the conversation, both literally and figuratively. By the beginning of the twentieth century, the increasing importance assigned to health and education for women gradually influenced the dominant discourse about middle-class female physicality. Women's experiences and their telling stories of their own experiences affected the discourse, which gradually shifted to suggest that women could exercise and study without these activities negatively affecting their childbearing capacity or the children themselves. Both good health and higher education were believed to be assets for (impending) motherhood. It was assumed that women who were healthy and well educated would be better mothers than those who lacked in either or both areas (Hargreaves, 1994). This was obviously a middle-class discourse because it excluded women who lacked the resources to go to college. Because women had to be strong enough to withstand the rigors of a higher education, physical education and sporting activities were part of the early curricula at the Seven Sister colleges, pioneers in the education of American women.

In contrast to how sport has been construed for men, women's sport was framed primarily as developmental, not competitive.[1] Educators went to great lengths to curb competitive sport for women because such physicality might masculinize female participants and would blur the required distinctions between women and men. As we showed earlier, a desirable form of masculinity was associated with competitiveness and physical toughness; real men displayed these qualities. Consequently, proper women were not supposed to show these qualities. Thus, only sport participation, not competition, was considered to be healthy for women. Women were still assumed to be muscularly weak and unable to run long distances and withstand the rigors of competition. A further difference between the meanings of sport for women and men is that there is little evidence that sport was used as a tool for evangelical outreach to women or that sport participation was assumed to make real women out of girls.

Meanings of sport that constructed women's physicality as relatively weak and limited prevailed into the 1970s and were used to keep women from participating in certain sport events such as the marathon, pole vault, rugby, boxing, wrestling, and so forth. In addition, well into the twentieth century, people assumed that women should not participate in sports or physical education during their menstrual periods because doing so was thought to put their uterus at risk. A vigorous sport such as basketball would be out for a menstruating woman because her uterus was understood to be "physiologically congested and temporarily abnormally heavy and hence, liable to displacement by the inexcusable strenuosity and roughness of this game" (quoted in Gerber, 1974, p. 16). Negative attitudes toward competitive and strenuous activity for women were not confined to the United States, but were part of a dominant discourse in the Western world and often just accepted as wisdom or common sense.[2]

Interestingly, the dominant discourse about gender and sport existed side by side with a dominant Western societal discourse dating back to Aristotle that emphasized a dualism of body and mind. The mind was constructed as being housed in the body and superior to it. Men were associated with the mind and women with nature or the body. Yet, the dominant discourse about sport constructed men, not women, as natural athletes. In contrast, as we saw in the previous chapter, dominant Western discourse about race associates whites with the mind and blacks with the body, with the skills of many black athletes often ascribed to their natural ability. Logic based on the dominant dualistic discourses would seem to suggest that women and black athletes (men and women) would then be described as natural athletes. This has not happened with respect to women, however, and is an indicator of the social construction of sport discourses of power and control rather than care and cooperation and also of the ability of white, middle- to upper-class men to collectively hold on to the privileges associated with their skin color and gender. The contralogical construction of women as related to "nature" more than men and yet not seen as "natural athletes" illustrates another of the many paradoxes of gender.

Dominant discourses about health, fitness, and women's capabilities continue to influence discourses about the decorum of sport activities for women today. Such discourses reflect cultural determination and specificity. For example, aggression and competition are defined as desirable qualities for Dutch men, especially in sport settings (Knoppers & Anthonissen, 2001; Warner, 1995). In the Netherlands, the national sport of soccer is considered a rough and tough sport much better suited to men than to women. Men, not women, are assumed to possess the required physical aggressiveness, strength, speed, and competitiveness to play it well (Derks, 1999; Elling, 1999; Knoppers & Anthonissen, 2003; Knoppers & Elling, 2001). Some Dutch coaches go so far as to insist that female bodies are not made for playing skillful soccer. A Dutch soccer coach explains, "in heading and other maneuvers you have to use different parts of the body. A woman's body is not designed to perform these skills well." Another coach argues that "a woman's body is best suited for other sports than soccer. Soccer can best be played by men" (Knoppers & Bouman, 1996, p. 92).

In other words, these Dutch men define soccer in ways that permit them to differentiate themselves from certain femininities. The contrasting meanings given to women's soccer in the United States, as described in the opening of the previous chapter, illustrate how context affects meaning. Although initially there was little acceptance of American women who participated in soccer, that resistance was part of the overall resistance to women's participation in competitive sports generally and was not tied to soccer specifically. The passage of Title IX in 1972[3] meant that the resistance to American women who played competitive sports began to decrease. In 1977, 2.8 percent of NCAA colleges and universities offered women's soccer; by 2008, that percent skyrocketed to 92 percent (Acosta & Carpenter, 2008). In distinction to the Netherlands, in the United States, coordination, speed, and stamina are offered as the most important success factors for soccer: "It is physical but not violent, demanding but not requiring exceptional size, bulk or upper body strength" (Henry & Comeaux, 1999, p. 278). In the States, soccer is seen as a sport that is played successfully by all body sizes and requires strategy and finesse more than brute strength. It is perceived to be a no-contact and gender-neutral sport requiring a quick mind (Andrews, 1999).

As the emphasis in discourses about American soccer is neither on the giving and taking of pain nor on being physically aggressive, it is not surprising that the media rarely use male American professional soccer players as displaying a desirable American masculinity. Sugden (1994), in a reflective essay about men's soccer, suggests that because soccer is seen as a women's sport in the United States, people do not take men's soccer seriously. He says, "That American women play the game so well and in such large numbers supports the view that men's soccer is a game for second-rate athletes who are unable to contend with the masculine rigors of the home-grown variety of football" (p. 249). He argues that the greater the popularity of women's soccer, the less likely it is that men's soccer will ever become a major sport in the States.

This comparison illustrates a general finding that men who wish to differentiate themselves from femininities often use a sport that has been defined as major or national in a country (Knoppers, 1999). A national sport, therefore, tends to be seen as a male sport although women may play it as well. This is true of ice hockey in Canada, football in the United States, soccer in the Netherlands, rugby in Western Australia, cricket in India, and so forth. In other words, despite women's entrance into competitive sport, the meanings given to national sports have changed little. They still tend to be used as a way for men, regardless of race or class, to differentiate themselves from what they define as effeminate.

If women and men were placed in equitable relation to one another in sport contexts, then paradoxes such as the preceding example, where soccer is defined as masculine in Europe and feminine in the United States, would fade. Qualities of cooperation as well as competition, of development as well as winning would coexist. Men's play and women's play of the same sport would be celebrated, with any differences between their play celebrated in the context of their similarities as athletes, rather than their distinctions highlighted as gendered.

Just as in men's sport, social class, race, and sexuality all play roles in definitions of appropriate sport participation for women.

SOCIAL CLASS

Social class shapes meanings given to sport and also influences who participates in sport. As indicated earlier, social class plays a role in defining which masculinities emerge in which sports. However, in the case of women, social class is a strong factor in determining the appropriateness of sport for women in general. During most of the nineteenth century, middle-class women were not allowed to participate in strenuous physical activity that might make them sweat. This reasoning was based on social-class differentiation between middle- and upper-class women and working-class women. Working-class women always were active and sweating as they worked long days in physically demanding jobs such as working in the fields; scrubbing floors and clothes; carrying heavy buckets; and operating heavy machinery, including large, hot kitchen stoves (Cahn, 1994). At the beginning of the twentieth century when physical activities gradually began to be considered healthy for women, participation was confined to those activities associated with leisure pursuits by the upper classes. As Cahn (1994) says, "The notion that 'refined' women played suitably 'refined' games protected elite sportswomen from violating the boundary between proper woman-hood and 'vulgar' women of other classes" (p. 15). It is not surprising, then, that the acceptance of women came more quickly in some sports than others. The middle- to upper-class associations with ski culture, and therefore with snowboarding, may explain why more women snow-board than participate in any other extreme sport.

In contrast, the acceptance of women's team sports associated with the white, male, working class has been slow. Sports that working-class men played have been defined as "vulgar," with no more logical reason than that they were played by working-class men and defined as requiring much physical strain and muscularity. Prior to the 1970s, these sports, therefore, were defined as being incongruent with white Western ideals of dominant forms of femininities (Cahn, 1994; Hargreaves, 1994; Pfister, Fasting, Scraton, & Vasquez, 1999). The working-to middle-class status of men's soccer in the Netherlands, for example, partially explains Dutch resistance to the growth of women's soccer (Knoppers & Anthonissen, 2003). In contrast, soccer started in the United States as a white, suburban, middle-class game, accounting per-haps for the acceptance given to female participation.

Not only soccer but other sports associated with the upper class such as tennis, golf, and snowboarding have tended to be more welcoming to female participants than sports associated with the lower-middle class such as wrestling, boxing, and skateboarding, where women had to fight to be allowed to participate in organized competition (Cahn, 1994; Hargreaves, 1994; Karsten & Pels, 2000; Knoppers & Anthonis-sen, 2003). Tennis and golf, the first two women's professional sports, and swimming, one of the first women's Olympic sports, had their competitive origins in sport clubs dominated by the white upper class in many countries in the Western world. Upper-class women played them because these sports were seen as games that were played devel-opmentally, as well as for fun and fresh air, and seemingly did not re-quire muscularity and aggressiveness. Ipso facto, these sports were also defined as ladylike because upper-class women played them (Derks, 1999; Hargreaves, 2000). Similarly, the suburban middle-class status of youth soccer made it acceptable for American women to play it without condemnation and, conversely, the participation of white middle-class women reinforced its status as a middle-class sport in the United States. Thus, class-related definitions have reinforced dominant beliefs and images about which sports were acceptable for women.

RACE

Not only class, but race also has been embedded in the definitions of appropriate sport participation for women. Most of the written history of women's sport participation has focused on white, middle-class women and the obstacles they faced. Definitions of womanhood have generally been more fluid in African American than in Euro-American communities (for varieties of reasons going back to slavery and continuing, often due to poverty and general racism that blocks African American women from the considerations of appropriateness applied to Euro-American women), and as a result, African American women have traditionally been less confined by narrow definitions of women's physicality than have white women (Cahn, 1994). This has meant that black women athletes who participated in sports such as track and field in the 1950s often received black community support while their white counterparts often received resistance and sometimes, outright condemnation for their participation. The obstacles that African American women athletes encountered came more frequently from white than from black men and women. White racist thought has constructed not only black men but also black women as natural athletes (Cahn, 1994). Thus, black women were allowed to participate in certain sports, even though the extent of their participation was circumscribed by Jim Crow laws and prejudice. Black tennis players, such as Olympic champions Althea Gibson and Arthur Ashe, encountered much prejudice, especially because tennis was considered to be a white middle- to upper-class sport. Due to race and class prejudice, middle-class sports were more accessible to women than were sports associated with the working class, while the reverse was true for black women.

These examples show that it is almost impossible to limit the analysis of meanings given to gender in relation to sport only to gender. At all times, gender is situated in intersecting social relationships. The relatively greater acceptance of black women in athletics generally, compared to the particular case of tennis, for example, is partially due to the intersections of class and race. Sport participation by black women in basketball, for example, a sport that was associated with the working class, has been more acceptable to the white middle-class establishment than is the participation of black women in tennis.[4] Yet, there are shared aspects of gender that are experienced by both black and white women athletes. Regardless of skin color and class, they may be trivialized and ignored by the media, by sponsors, and by sport consumers (Cahn, 1994).

Intersections of race and gender can play out in other ways as well. Banet-Weiser (1999) has explored the various ways in which the NBA and WNBA are represented in media discourses. A popular image of the NBA has been of a league dominated by black male individualists who are perceived to be troublemakers and not always worth the money that has been paid for them. In contrast, the WNBA, also with its share of black players, has been marketed as a league where basketball is a wholesome and healthy family activity. Banet-Weiser says, "This 'different attitude' resides in the bodies of female players, indeed it is the bodies of the players, bodies that are more moral, more pure, less likely to succumb to temptation, and less corrupt than male bodies" (p. 416).

Banet-Weiser also notes that WNBA women tend to be presented as strong, competitive, and aggressive. Thus, representations of these women basketball players both challenge and confirm gender and racial stereotypes simultaneously. Meanings given to sexuality play a role here as well, however.

SEXUALITY

The sexuality of athletic women has always been part of the meanings given to their sport participation, though differently from men's sport. This difference shows how meanings given to competitive physicalities often contradict and complicate each other. Media depictions of women athletes focus on their sexuality, portraying them as mothers and/or sex objects and bringing to the fore questions about their sexual orientation. The fact that various women basketball players are mothers has received a great deal of positive press and ensures that these athletes are marketed as mature women, not as sex objects. The women of the WNBA, regardless of their race, serve not only as alternative role models to the NBA but also to the dominant manner in which the media present women athletes.

This is not the case in other media depictions of women athletes, however. More often than not, women's sexual attractiveness, rather than their athletic abilities, gains media attention. Sexually provocative sights, such as nude bungee jumping, scantily dressed female wrestlers, and skimpily clad women in the stands at men's sporting events often receive more attention than coverage of regular women's sports. The annual swimsuit issue of *Sports Illustrated* exemplifies this emphasis (Davis, 1997). Year after year, *Sports Illustrated* pays more attention to women in its annual swimsuit issue than it does to competitive women athletes in all its regular issues combined. This is part of a trend in which the media focus on female athletes whom they consider to be heterosexually attractive, talk about the boyfriends of these athletes and their dependence on males, and pay attention to the lives of these athletes outside of sport in ways markedly dissimilar from male athletes.[5]

The attention given to tennis player Anna Kournikova is illustrative. She had never won a major tournament and yet had earned about ten million dollars a year for endorsements (Messner, 2002). This is not to say that female tennis players should not be watched nor receive endorsements for their physical attractiveness but that less stereotypically attractive women athletes with better skills do not get those endorsements. Both good looking and ugly men in men's sports get their share of endorsements because of their athletic skills and prowess; in women's sports the lion's share of media attention and endorsements tends to go to those seen as heterosexually attractive. This emphasis on perceived sexual attractiveness of female athletes to men has implications for every woman who participates in competitive sports, particularly at the elite level and has its roots in historical processes.

In the first half of the twentieth century, societal gender stereotyping included a gradual blending of gender and sexuality. A man who displayed what was assumed to be part of heterosexual femininity was seen as effeminate or gay; a woman who acted in a mannish manner was assumed to be lesbian. This blending of gender and sexuality plus the increasing emphasis on sport as a manly endeavor in the nineteenth and twentieth centuries has translated into explicit homophobia and heterosexism in women's sport. The societal association between strong women athletes (that is, those who play "like men") and lesbians has increased since the beginning of the twentieth century. The dominant fear about competitive women in the early 1900s was that competitive sport would masculinize them. In the twenty-first century, the fear is that women's sports, especially those associated with men, are dominated by lesbians and lesbianize women.[6] This association could intimidate any woman athlete who does not fit neatly into the meanings given to desirable femininities. Ironically, members of sport organizations and institutions, especially those in the United States, have not identified homophobia or heterosexism but, rather, lesbian participation as a growing problem in women's sport (Griffin, 1998), thereby slicing off an entire group of people, rather than addressing a harmful ideology.

The growing demonization of lesbian athletes in the last several decades, especially in the United States, has meant that female athletes may spend a great deal of time proving that they fit the heterosexual stereotype: They have boyfriends, wear their long hair in pony tails, and wear makeup outside (and sometimes inside) the gym (Cahn, 1994; Kolnes, 1995; Lenskij, 1986). Title IX was passed in the early 1970s at the time when the gay and lesbian rights movement began to grow. The success of this movement meant that homosexuality began to receive more societal attention and therefore, became more visible. This was happening while female athletes and coaches were trying to prove that sport did not make them mannish, a quality associated with being lesbian. Consequently, lesbian athletes, especially in the States, have faced an increasingly hostile environment. Many leaders of women's sport have been afraid that this attention would negatively influence the growing interest and public support for women's sport and, consequently, often failed to support lesbian athletes and coaches (Hall, M. A., 1996). While the gay and lesbian movement emphasized gay pride and coming out, lesbian athletes and coaches did their best to pass as straight, and heterosexuals did their best to show they were not lesbian. Thus, many female athletes were and continue to be affected by homophobia and heterosexism.

This demonizing of women athletes who fit a certain stereotype still occurs today although there are more female athletes, particularly in individual sports such as tennis and golf, who are open about being lesbian (Hargreaves, 2002). Again, the sports associated with the middle to upper class seem to be the first to provide more acceptance to those thought of as deviant. Although Martina Navratilova lost many endorsements after she came out of the closet, she continued to play and to serve as a model for other lesbians. Most lesbian athletes and coaches, especially those in team sports, however, continue to play it safe and stay in the closet. A noticeable exception is Sheryl Swoopes, an African American WNBA player, often considered to be the Michael Jordan of women's basketball, who came out in 2005. Such is the complexity of meanings given to women in sport that her coming out was not considered a media event, unlike an equivalent coming out of a celebrated male athlete. Zirin (2005) argues that most sports writers assume that most female athletes are lesbian.

At the same time, the label *lesbian* can be used to discredit coaches in recruiting battles for the best female athletes. By accusing a coach of being lesbian, opposing coaches can use this fear to induce recruits to come and play at their safe institution. As Griffin (1998) argues:

> It matters little whether or not the women accused are lesbians. Such lesbian baiting is used to discredit strong women in or out of sport. Hillary Rodham Clinton, Janet Reno, and Donna Shalala are all women in powerful positions who have been called lesbians in an attempt to discredit them. (p. 61)

The history of women's sport has shown that there always have been issues about women's participation that have nothing to do with the exhilaration of a superbly played shot or exceeding one's personal best. According to Griffin (1998), sexually discrediting women athletes and coaches is a powerful tool that can be used to control women's sport. The power attached to this image of a lesbian as boogey woman depends on the context and/or country and type of sport. In a country such as the Netherlands, most incidents of discrimination against lesbians occur in women's soccer (Elling, de Knop, & Knoppers, 2003; Hekma, 1994). Managers of some Dutch soccer clubs do not want women's teams because they are afraid such teams will consist of and attract lesbians; a lesbian image might be bad for the club. Ironically, this happens in a country well known for its tolerance and acceptance of gays and lesbians. Thus, global meanings given to intersections of gender and sport may at times be stronger than local norms and values. Sports that are allied most closely with male heterosexuality, such as soccer in most countries and team sports in general in the United States, are sports that most overtly discredit and resist gays and lesbians. While the heterosexuality of men who are outstanding in sport is assumed (sometimes wrongly), sport participation for outstanding females is often seen as synonymous with homosexuality, especially in male-dominated sports.

Ironically, this demonization of gays and lesbians in sport is based on simplistic forms of stereotyping. There are women who can look heterosexually attractive and be lesbians and women who are assumed to be lesbians who are heterosexual (Caudwell, 1999), just as men who can outperform and outmuscle their male opponents can be gay (Anderson, E., 2000; Klein, 1993). Yet, meanings assigned to sport and its participants continue to strengthen and reinforce these simplistic dualisms.

Thus, women's sport provides ways in which class, race, and sexuality differentiate the performance of women and at the same time provides examples of ways in which those intersections can shift. Obviously, the history of women's sport has changed the meanings that people give to white, middle-class women as being weak and unable to participate in strenuous physical activity besides childbearing. Women continue to challenge the boundaries of the meanings given to their physicality. In doing so, women claim agency and space for sharing stories and experiences that may change the sport system, enacting a stake in that system, taking care of themselves.

TRANSGENDERED ATHLETES

Further complicating the story of gender and sport is integration of transgendered people and their athleticism. We have used men's and women's sporting practices to illustrate paradoxes in meanings given to masculinity and femininity at various levels and how they trouble or disrupt seemingly common sense notions about the relationship between male and masculinity and female and femininity. Although the focus of this book is not on the classification of people into the gender categories of male and female but on the meanings we give to those categories, the formal structure of sport into men and women's sport also requires stability of the gender binary of male and female.

At the beginning of the previous chapter's discussion about men's sport we showed how the fear of the perceived feminization of society motivated those designing curricula for elite boys' schools to include sport. This fear and other related societal dynamics resulted in the formal organization of many sports including the Olympic games. As the Olympic games became professionalized, participation in them was organized on the basis of countries as well as on gender. This meant that individual performances were linked to national pride and seen as a way of "defeating" other nations.

Women from Western countries, especially the USA, dominated the early games and won most of the medals in the category of women's sport (Cahn, 1994; Cavanagh & Sykes, 2006). During the Cold War, however, women from Eastern bloc countries challenged this status quo. Officials from Western countries such as the USA became concerned that their dominance in these games was threatened by the outstanding performances of women athletes from Eastern European countries. Although by today's standards, their performances rank as average for elite athletes, at that time, Eastern European athletes' results were considered to be impossible for women to achieve. In addition, the bodies of elite Eastern European countries, although fitting into today's image of many elite female athletes, did not fit the stereotypical ideas about what a "feminine" body should look like at that time.

The International Olympic Committee (chaired by an American, Avery Brundage) suspected that these "impossible" performances and body types meant that these women must be men and were therefore not deserving of the medals they received. Consequently, in 1968, the IOC introduced sex testing for women athletes to protect "true" women athletes from unfair competition. The required sex testing initially was based on an examination of external genitalia; subsequently the test was based on chromosomal evidence, that is, it assumed that those classified as "real women" could only have XX chromosomes. Men were not subjected to this sex test since no conceivable advantage could be imagined for a woman to participate in a men's competition. Transsexuals or transgender people in general or those participating in men's sports were obviously not deemed worthy of such "protection."

As we suggested in the birthing chapter, determining a person's sex is not as straightforward as it may seem. Is it based on genitalia? Chromosomes? Hormonal levels? The sex a person thinks s/he is? Sex testing for international sport competitions was fraught with the same difficulties. The results of chromosomal testing revealed that several women athletes with female genitalia possessed a chromosomal makeup of XXY. The IOC judged that those possessing such chromosomes were not officially women although there is little evidence that chromosomal makeup directly impacts performance (Cahn, 1994; Gooren 2008). In addition, not only physiological but also many mental, cultural, and social factors influence performance, which may explain why women with XX chromosomes currently are breaking the records set by Eastern bloc participants in the past. In addition, this criterion did not provide any guidelines for transgender athletes whose chromosomal makeup and gender identity did not match. Gradually it became obvious that a definitive test of gender identity does not exist, so that the IOC ceased sex testing in 2000.

In 2004 the IOC agreed that transsexuals could compete in the Olympics under certain conditions[7] and at the same time, reserved the right to order testing of anyone whose gender identity fell under "suspicion."[8] Once again such suspicion is related to meanings given to gender as the case of Kathy Jager illustrates (Pilgrim, Martin, & Binder, 2003). Kathy Jager broke the 100 meter record in track for her age group (she was 56 at the time) during the 1999 World Veterans Championship. Another athlete was suspicious of Jager's accomplishment, her body build, and her explosive strength and accused her of being male. As a result, and although she had birthed two children, Jager had to undergo a sex test. The results indicated that she was born a female.

Thus regardless of the number of female athletes currently participating in sport, their muscularity can still be a reason to question their gender identity! In other words, well-defined muscularity is still assumed to be an inherent or "natural" part of (heterosexual) masculinity. There is no history of male athletes being forced to undergo sex testing because they are very graceful and flexible, two physical components often associated with women, or because they are seen as "playing like a bunch of girls" as was the case of a Dutch male soccer team (Knoppers, 1999).

Although the discourse that assumes congruence between male and masculinity and between female and femininity has been challenged in many ways, it still is powerful. The IOC's 2004 decision to permit transgender athletes to participate in its events is an example of how seemingly unchangeable/natural categorization practices can be challenged, and at the same time the restrictions accompanying this decision show how change is limited when "old" discourses are used to justify or circumvent it. Ironically, although the use of modern training methods, technology, and changes in various sports such as bodybuilding have shown that assumptions about the definition of a 'natural' body are continually changing, various discourses still reflect the assumption that a natural performing body is a static entity that can be universally defined and classed as male/masculine and female/femininity. Perhaps the continued use of such discourses reflects more a desire to have bodies and gender neatly defined and classified/matched than that it reflects the variation in embodied lives.

REFLECTIONS

It is clear that sport has been given meanings that intersect with gender, social class, race, and sexuality. These meanings shift as women also persist, enter every sport, and give new meanings to femininities. These meanings often overlap with those given to masculinities, and their meanings vary across race, social class, and sexuality. The success of the tennis playing Williams sisters, for example, disrupts both class and race boundaries. At the same time their success may also confirm stereotypes about the physicality of black women. The coming out of Sheryl Swoopes and John Amaechi challenge dominant meanings given to race, gender, and sexuality in different ways while at the same time confirming other meanings about blacks and about the sexuality of female athletes in team sports (Zirin, 2005).

We have also shown in this chapter the impact of women's sports on definitions given to femininity outside of sport. Women have more opportunities than they did 150 years ago to exercise their athletic, physical, and mental gifts and strengths and increasingly do so. How long will men then be able to use men's sports to differentiate themselves from what is associated with womanly? We have argued that meanings given to sports continually shift and new sports continue to be created by boys to create new masculinities.[9] It is possible that men's sport could become less interesting to many men than it is now if it were not a place where distinctions are drawn on the bases of gender and sexuality. On the other hand, the number of women and men who refuse to be complicit in the differentiation between women and men and simultaneously between gay and lesbian could increase so that the coming out of the closet of elite athletes is no longer worth a news headline. The visibility of gay and lesbian athletes could change derogatory meanings given to gay and lesbian outside of sport and the necessity of distinguishing between manly and womanly, thereby enhancing the humanity of athletes rather than their sexual constitution.

Thus, an ethic of care elbows its way into the sport arena. When room is created or found or claimed by people, even ones with lower power in a system, and when mutuality shows itself, even in constrained ways, human caring, leading to more equitable treatment of people, develops.

NOTES

1. See Cahn, 1994; Hargreaves, 1994; and Lenskij, 1986, for a detailed history of women in sport.

2. See for example, Derks, 1999.

3. Title IX is a federal law that is part of the Education Amendments of 1972 to the Civil Rights Act of 1964. It prohibits sex discrimination against students and employees of educational institutions and states that "No person in the United States shall, on the basis of sex, be excluded from participation in, or denied the benefits of, or be subjected to discrimination under any educational program or activity receiving federal assistance." For further details see www .american.edu/sadker/titleix.htm.

4. The advent of Venus and Serena Williams has changed the white face of tennis to a certain degree. Much of the media coverage constructs them as exotic women and in turn, the Williams sisters cultivate that image. It is possible that black tennis players need to have something extra and/or be super good in order to make it in the white, upper-class tennis world. For media analysis of the Williams sisters and racism in tennis, see Stevenson, 2002 and Spencer, 2004.

5. See for example, Hargreaves, 2000; Kolnes, 1995; Longman, 2001; Messner, 2002.

6. See Cahn, 1994; Griffin, 1998; Hargreaves, 2000, for more in-depth discussion of this development.

7. "sex reassignment must have taken place at least two years earlier, hormone treatment must be appropriate for the reassigned sex and the reassigned sex must be legally recognized" (Gooren, 2008, p. 427). In addition, current anti-doping policies may prevent a female-to-male transsexual from participating in elite competition since testosterone therapy is part of his treatment.

8. The IOC reserves the right to carry out a sex-test (called suspicion-based testing) if the gender of an athlete is questioned (Pilgrim, Martin, and Binder, 2003).

9. It is possible that physical activities that girls engage in will not be considered as sports because girls are not associated with sport.

5

BODIES AT WORK

Masculinities, Management, and Physicality

Whenever an American workman plays baseball, or an English workman plays cricket, it is safe to say that he strains every nerve to secure victory for his side. He does his very best to make the largest possible number of runs. The universal sentiment is so strong that any man who fails to give out all there is in him in sport is branded as a "quitter," and treated with contempt by those who are around him.

When the same workman returns to work on the following day, instead of using every effort to turn out the largest possible amount of work, in a majority of the cases this man deliberately plans to do as little as he safely can. (Taylor, 1911, p. 5)

Being tough, disciplined, and physically strong enough to dominate others often is the central criterion for evaluating everyone from coaches to business executives: "doing it like a man" is usually the way to gain power and influence. (Coakley, 2007, p. 268)

Participation in sports can significantly shape managerial interactions and indeed career progress . . . as men try to relate toward each other as colleagues, employees, clients and customers, competitors and teammates. (Collinson & Hearn, 1996, p. 4)

When I get to the top, there will be corporate shopping
days and corporate cooking classes, corporate massage
days!! No more yachting, no more rugby, no more
cricket. (Pringle, 2004, p. 89)

As we indicated in previous chapters, physicality, especially as developed through sport, plays a highly visible role in society and in meanings given to gender. Meanings given to gender in sport migrate into constructions of gender in many other aspects of life, such as the paid work world. For some workers, physicality is a job requirement. Construction workers, luggage handlers, and health care workers, to name just a few, use their bodies in their professions. Others, however, such as civil servants, ministers, and teachers, seem to be able to do their jobs no matter what their gender or level of fitness may be. This appears to be especially true of management.

Managers rarely engage in the primary physical activity of an organization. Instead, they do work that does not require physical prowess, such as showing leadership and developing strategic direction for the organization and personnel. In addition to appearing far removed from physical exertion, managerial tasks seem to be gender neutral. It seems this is one part of the world where one's skills, talents, and abilities would matter more than one's gender. The paradox, however, is that meanings given to sport and gender that privilege masculinity also matter in managerial activities and in meanings given to the position of manager. Physically fit or not, masculine or not, managers find that their work implicates both.

Congruencies among management, gender, and sport are rooted in conditions found in the beginnings of both organized sport and management in the mid-nineteenth century. Created by men for men, management and sport continue to be dominated numerically and culturally by hegemonic forms of masculinity. Additionally, the higher the position, the greater is the probability that the manager is a man. In the United States, for example, men make up 89 percent of the corporate executive officers and 97.3 percent of the top earners in the Fortune 500 companies ("Statistics—Women," n.d.). Even within the more evenly balanced middle management and administrative jobs, the gender ratio still favors men. No matter whether women outnumber men in activities and jobs such as in churchgoing and nursing, even there, men remain the majority of managers and leaders.

Much research has focused on exploring the paradox (given that there is no real need of maleness or physical strength) of women's scarcity in executive management positions. While we will discuss this research in the following section, the more compelling questions are: why are so many managers and/or leaders male? To what extent is the numerical and cultural dominance of men connected with meanings given to the body and physicality? To what extent do discourses about managerial work and about athletic masculinities overlap? What would it take to create a working climate in which women and men would thrive well? These questions apply also to leadership positions in general. Dominant discourses cluster together, showing the hegemonic power of the discourses of masculinity and physicality in arenas where money and authority matter. We begin the exploration with a look at the context of the conceptual origin of management, where (similar to the case in sport) the discourses and practices of *manager* were tied to a certain type of men and masculinity.[1]

HISTORY OF MANAGEMENT AND GENDER

The job of manager first emerged during the Industrial Revolution, when factories and businesses were expanding rapidly (Hearn, 1998). The frenetic pace of industrial expansion required owners to hire others to run and control their businesses. Evocatively, the meaning of the verb *to manage* is rooted in the Italian word *menagerie* which means "handling things, especially horses" (Collinson & Hearn, 1996, p. 2). From the start, managers experienced ambiguous expectations and conflicting loyalties. What skills are managers required to have? How should they do their work? To what extent are they responsible for organizational outcomes and employee behavior? Where should the loyalties of the manager lie—with the owner, or the employees, and/or the production process? These elements of ambiguity meant that a central discourse-related role of management would be to control uncertainty.

Middle- to upper-class men created a culture of management congenial to men like themselves. Assuming that managers had wives at home to run their households and raise their children, a key expectation for managers was that they would devote most of their time and energy to their jobs.[2] Although much of the day-to-day work of management has changed since its early days, the assumption of almost total availability (and geographic mobility) of managers and others in positions of leadership remains embedded in its structure today, being seen as a self-evident requirement of the job.

The early literature on management employed masculine military and sport metaphors and experiences, describing managers and/or leaders as heroic men (Hearn, 1989; Wajcman, 1998). One of the first management scientists, Frederick Taylor (1911), tried to reduce management work to a system. Scientific management emphasizes rationality, control, discipline, and mastery over self and others. As the chapter's opening quote highlights, Taylor used baseball coaching as an example of how managers should work. It was up to the manager to make sure employees worked as hard in the organization or business as they did on the baseball field. The mechanistic perspective of Taylorism, where employees were seen as fungible and managers as motivators, still plays a role today. Current variations of the mechanistic perspective include management by objectives (MBO) and planning, programming, and budgeting systems (PPBS). These Tayloristic approaches, emphasizing control and external motivation, contrast starkly with more caring approaches that would treat managers and employees alike as full human beings. Tayloristic approaches require employees to adjust to the demands and wishes of management and are assumed to increase efficiency and therefore productivity.

Gradually however, the mechanistic way of managing began to be questioned. In the 1920s, primary emphasis in management practices gradually began to shift from organizational needs to include the needs of employees. It was now assumed that managers should not only ensure collectivity but also facilitate workers' personal growth in order to enhance productivity. This approach to management became known as the human relations approach, and it has become part of what is now called systems theory. In the 1980s, the human relations approach advocated controlling people through human resource management (HRM) and controlling the organization through total quality management (TQM). These ways of managing uncertainty by controlling people and organizations were rooted in American adaptations of Japanese management styles (Wajcman, 1998).

Human resource management encourages managers to create a cohesive organizational culture by using a style that incorporates positive leadership, develops a sense of teamwork among employees, and secures their commitment to the organization. This type of management requires managers to have a so-called people orientation, which fosters shared visions, values, and responsibilities to the end goal of productivity. Because a people orientation has traditionally been primarily associated with women, HRM managerial styles have been assumed to help create more women-friendly organizational cultures and managerial leadership styles. To a certain degree, this assumption has been realized in middle management, where more and more women find work. However, when it comes to top management, women continue to be in the minority. The HRM approach seemingly has made very small openings for women in organizational structures of leadership. Variations of both Taylorism and human needs approaches to management seem to assume (erroneously) that managers are usually men and/or that management theories are gender neutral.[3]

Managerial Women

The slow increase in the presence of senior women managers has meant that research on gender and management has focused primarily on women managers, rather than on gender theory more broadly defined as social and cultural, rather than just personal.[4] Researchers have explored mechanisms and influences that keep women in lower management positions and that exclude them from higher positions. The results usually attribute the relative lack of women managers in higher positions to a mismatch between organizational and family-time demands; to gendered structures of managerial work, including exclusion from vital networks; and to (a lack of) personal competencies. In other words, the research tends to blame qualities and characteristics most often associated with women for the failure of women to progress in management, thereby blaming the victims. The new rhetoric of human resource management and people orientation makes it seem that management is now wide open to women, and if they are not represented equally there, it is because of their own decisions. In addition, many organizations work toward being equal-opportunity employers and recruit women aggressively. The paradox remains that although recruitment procedures have become more inclusive, most of those selected for high-level positions still tend to be (white) men. Several factors may play a role in the presence of this paradox.

One factor underlying the gendered selection process may be related to the element of uncertainty that pervades managerial work. Due to the importance of the work and the uncertainty about how well a manager might do, people select managers who look like the ones who were successful in the past. Further, Kanter (1977) has shown how managers tend to select people like themselves for positions of power. Essed (2002), a Dutch anthropologist, names the preference for masculine, white, and European men for positions of leadership, "cultural cloning." Men who fit this normative profile are assumed to be reliable because they look and act like the men already there, and these sorts of people are perceived as able to subordinate demands of the home to those of work.

The effort to control uncertainty by selecting cultural clones can be seen clearly when organizations made up mostly of women are restructured, with new senior positions created. For example, a study of organizational change in the health care sector shows the paradox of the fact that internal recruiting procedures used to select senior managers from a primarily female nursing staff resulted in the predominant selection of men for these positions (Kvande, 2002). Similarly, in a study of gendered processes in the selection of leaders in Norwegian sport organizations, Hovden (2000) finds that the rhetoric of selection discourses (such as advertising for the position and job descriptions) was based on heroic, masculine images of corporate leadership skills. In such a case, even though selection committees may profess to want women for certain positions, they often work consciously or subconsciously with a (white) male image of the ideal candidate.

Yet, as the statistics at the beginning of this chapter indicate, some women are selected to managerial positions. How did they obtain such positions? Often because, in some key ways, they are seen as masculine. In other words, although being a woman makes them an anomaly, their leadership styles and the manner in which they manage and carry out their responsibilities appear similar to those of (male) managers who already have senior-level positions (Claringbould, Knoppers, & Elling, 2004). Corporate and organizational boards of directors and management teams often want to hire women for high-level positions because it is seen as ethically correct to have at least one woman present and because women are assumed to bring something different to the position. Paradoxically, however, these women must be cultural clones of current management and CEOs. It is not surprising, then, that Wajcman (1998), in her study of senior managers in five multinationals, finds that there is no such thing as a distinctively female management style. In order for women to succeed, she concluded that they have to adopt a male style, especially at the senior managerial level. It is not surprising, then, that gender differences in managerial styles have been found primarily in lower- and middle-management positions, where the stakes are lower and where other women may be represented as decision-makers, though not in senior management positions.

A consequence of the unspoken, but still required, use of a normative masculine management style, especially at higher levels, means that women and men managers who work differently face a greater chance of being fired or of feeling forced out of their jobs. For women, no matter how much their lives reflect masculine norms (such as mobility and lack of home responsibilities), paradoxically people see them as being different from the norm of the male manager. Their bodies, even if masked in a suit and bow tie (as in the "dress for success" fashion of the 1980s), mark them as different and as anomalies. In some way, they just do not belong there. It is not surprising, then, that women often experience glass ceilings and walls and tend to leave organizations in higher numbers than their male counterparts.[5]

Implicitly, the idea exists that men literally, as well as figuratively, fit best in the rational culture of an efficient organization. In a study of Dutch senior managers, an executive director is quoted as explaining what happens in public-safety organizations where few women are in upper-level positions: "Women are the exception here. Everything they do receives a lot of scrutiny. The moment they make a mistake it becomes magnified and is used to confirm the prevailing belief that women are not suited for such a high position; and so they leave" (Knoppers & Anthonissen, 2004). According to Rutherford (2001), "Men's ability to hold onto management as a male domain is rooted in men's ability to construct the cluster of skills that make up management as being rooted in masculinity" (p. 328). In other words, as long as management and/or leadership remains associated with ways of working that are linked to certain ways of doing masculinity, corporate masculinity will continue to grant the advantage to men who fit that mold in relation to most women (and other men who do not fit the image) (Kerfoot & Knights, 1998; Maier, 1999; Whitehead, 2002; Whitehead & Barrett, 2001).

Despite at least thirty years of research and policy-making directed primarily at increasing the number of women senior managers, notwithstanding the so-called feminization of management through HRM, and, in spite of the changes in the way managers do their work, senior management remains primarily a male preserve, both numerically and culturally (Davidson & Burke, 2004; Hearn, 1998; Kerfoot & Knights, 1998; Reskin, 1988; Witz & Savage, 1992). Obviously, then, discourses about managerial skills and masculinities are related and require attention. Add to this mix the discourses about sport, and the relationships among masculinity construction, management, and sport that militate against a good fit between women and business management emerge more clearly.

Managerial Men

No single style of masculinity dominates management practices, although people generally associate the required skills, expectations, and attitudes with masculinity.[6] Managers can choose from a repertoire of styles and discourses. Collinson and Hearn's (1996) describe how senior managers act to provide connection points with sport. Three of these, entrepreneurialism, informalism, and careerism, find their corollaries in sport discourses.[7] These are not separate categories but, instead, are ways of managing. Sometimes they overlap; sometimes they even contradict each other. Taken together, though, analyses of these three in relation to sport reveal associations between managerial and athletic masculinities. We draw the examples in this section from ethnographic data on research with senior managers (Knoppers & Anthonissen, 2004, 2005, 2008; Knoppers, 2009).

Entrepreneurialism : Hardnosed and Competitive

Collinson and Hearn (1996) define entrepreneurialism in ways that resonate with sport. To begin, it can be described as acting businesslike; senior managers need to be hardnosed, guided by rational pragmatism, emotional neutrality, competitive spirit, focused on reaching targets, efficient, and work long hours.[8] Metaphors drawn from the sport world dominate this discourse. References to "scoring," "winning," "fumbling the ball," and "the ball is in their court" abound. Yet, the links between discourses about sport and business are greater than just the use of sport metaphors. Sport discourses frequently highlight the correlations among masculinity, competitiveness, and toughness (Connell, 2000). One senior manager who works for the police explains that "successful managing requires achievement just like sport" and another notes, "managing a division is like coaching a team." Both entrepreneurial and sport discourses value gung-ho rhetoric.

Direct overlap between sport and business-related discourses occurs in other ways as well. Many companies sponsor sporting events and athletes and/or host clients in skyboxes and luxury suites. Business transactions may be conducted in the stadium during a football or basketball game. Coakley (2007) explains that managerial attendance at a game celebrates and privileges the values and experiences of the men who control and benefit from corporate wealth and power in North America. This explains why men pay thousands of dollars to buy expensive season tickets to college and professional football games, why male executives use corporate credit cards to buy blocks of company tickets to football games, and why corporation presidents write hundred-thousand dollar checks to pay for luxury suites and club seats for themselves, friends, and clients. Football is entertaining for these spectators, but, more importantly, it reproduces a way of viewing the world that fosters their interests.

By using sports events as sites for business transactions, top executives show that they identify with the character and qualities of athletic masculinity. Because they are seen as more masculine, certain sports lend themselves better than others to management work. Executives are more likely to conduct business transactions during team sports such as football, basketball, and baseball and upper-class individual sports such as tennis and golf than while attending events such as gymnastics, figure skating, and synchronized swimming. Even when men perform in those sports, the association with hegemonic masculinity is lower. Therefore, not all types of athletic masculinities are associated with entrepreneurial discourses.

Because entrepreneurial discourse is shaped by emphases on attendance at and participation in men's professional sports events and/or using them to entertain clients (McDowell, 2001), it is not surprising, then, that this discourse draws heavily on sport metaphors and associations. The overlap between sport and business discourses requires a great deal of complicity from women and marginalized men who are managers. Ironically, women managers who cheer the heroic parts of sporting masculinities at a sporting event are celebrating behaviors that they themselves will rarely be allowed to show. If they do so, often there is a backlash. When women show the required competitive behavior that is part of this discourse, their behavior may be seen as conflicting with dominant notions about required femininity. The ability of women managers to be hardnosed and competitive is given different meanings and valued differently than when men engage in the same behaviors. In one case, the only female member of the board of directors of a national sport association explains how this works: "A man is not worth anything if he shows no ambition but about an ambitious women they say 'here we have another bitch'" (Claringbould & Knoppers, 2007, p. 68). Almost invisible because, after all, the woman is on the board, the taboo of a woman acting like a man is enforced by the trivializing comments of her male counterparts. Yet, while that taboo constrains women's power, paradoxically, male managers who care little about sport still may benefit from the privilege of being male and therefore be granted the assumption of male physical superiority by association.

In the business of sport itself, reciprocally, managers invoke the rhetoric of entrepreneurialism to argue why women are rarely invited to become top managers and/or coaches of top (male) teams (Knoppers & Bouman, 1998; Collinson & Hearn, 1994; McKay, 1997). Because they are women, they are assumed not to be aggressive, tough, or willing to work the long hours that are deemed to be necessary to do a good job.

The rhetoric of entrepreneurialism deftly blames women themselves for their relative absence from high managerial positions. No matter what the actual case may be, women are perceived as uninterested in the aggressive parts of managerial life. Consequently, they tend to be hired for what are seen as soft jobs such as human resource management and public relations. Complementary, even symbiotic, relations exist between discourses of sport and entrepreneurialism. These discourses put most men in a place of privilege while simultaneously excluding women and also, to a lesser degree, men who value different ways of doing masculinity and managerial work.

Informalism or Networking: Space for Male Bonding

Collinson & Hearn (1996) name informalism as another discursive practice used in managerial work; this old boys' network draws on assumed shared male interests and common values. Noting its intrinsically exclusionary nature, they argue, "Within these informal relationships, men are often concerned to identify with other men in the 'in-group,' while simultaneously differentiating themselves from other groups of men and from women" (Collinson & Hearn, 1996, p. 159). Similarity and difference play a role in who is counted as in or out. Those who are judged to be different from white men, such as ethnic minorities and women, often are excluded. A male minority manager explains: "Now that I have proved myself I can be different; in general it is difficult to be different because it is held against you" (Knoppers & Anthonissen, 2004). The dynamics of these networks reflect what is sometimes described as a locker-room culture that supports managerial discourses that emphasize emotional detachment, competitiveness, and the sexual objectification of women (Bird, 1996; Collinson & Hearn, 1996).

Given the term "locker-room culture," it is not surprising that men's elite team and individual sports play a large role in networking practices. Men may develop skills through playing sports in high school or college that later will enhance informalist practices as they learn to relate to their colleagues, customers, employees, and competitors. Further, watching or engaging in sport while doing business (entrepreneurial discourse), but also talking about it (informalist discourse) creates shared experiences and interests. For example, one of the most popular topics for informal discussions among those involved in the European Commission besides food and/or wine, is soccer (Woodward, 1996). A senior manager in New Zealand describes how essential it is to be part of this talk: "So if you're not going to be drinking beer and talking about rugby with the boys, sometimes you miss out on critical conversation . . . work will come up and they will make a decision in your absence" (Pringle, 2004, p. 91).

Talking about sport allows men to create acceptable social intimacy with each other as they describe their personal experiences in sport and their reasons for (not) cheering for certain players or teams (Kiesling, 2003). The ability to engage in informal sport discourse helps men transcend organizational boundaries, allowing them to enter into easy conversations at professional occupational meetings and at sporting events in their professional capacities. Conversely, male managers who show little interest in national men's sports (or sport in general) and/or who have little or no competitive sport history, tend to be excluded from these entrepreneurial practices that are the "core of corporate culture" (Coakley, 2007, p. 367; Pronger, 1999).

Curiously, informalist discourses and practices allow men to engage in something usually relegated to women: emotional intimacy. While doing or talking about sport, male managers are able to enhance their networks and their bonding with other men because they are in a heteronormative space where their sexual orientation is not in question and, so, a certain degree of emotional intimacy is permissible (McDowell 2001; Roper, 1996). According to Roper (1996), "Intimacies between male managers are crucially important, however, because it is through them that 'exclusionary circles' are formed and maintained" (p. 224). Thus, these sport-related spaces provide opportunities for male managers to differentiate themselves from women and from other men. Kerfoot and Knights (1998) explain that intimacy currently is considered a necessary part of managerial work: "Intimacy is seen to oil the wheels of communication as a necessary condition of securing outcomes that extend beyond the interests of any one individual" (p. 438). Thus, networks may be a place for both differentiation and for building intimate relationships.

Evoking sport events or talking sport may give managers permission to touch each other and to share certain joys and sorrows because the sport context is linked to that. The emphasis on heteronormativity in both sport and nonsport organizations may obscure the erotic and/or sexual nature of male homosociality while allowing male athletes and managers to experience pleasure in each other's company (Kerfoot & Knights, 1998; Moodley, 1999). Homosociality among male managers therefore may be shaped and strengthened by a shared passion for sport.[9] The presence of women and/or gay men, even when they are knowledgeable about sport, has the potential to disturb this heteronormative male intimacy and pleasure, perhaps by making it explicitly visible. What the men involved may prefer to understand as the touch of camaraderie may be interpreted primarily in a sexual way, that is, as a sexual advance. When women and openly gay men are part of this network, their presence may make these intimacies visible and may blur certain boundaries, exposing and thereby invoking the gender taboo of straight men identifying with women or with gay men.

Careerism: Being Better than the Rest

Careerism is the third discourse that shapes managerial work (Collinson & Hearn, 1996). This discourse emphasizes climbing organizational and professional ladders (hierarchical advancement), creating and reaching performance targets, and obtaining superior evaluations. Managers use these factors to compete with other managers and therefore to distinguish themselves from each other.

A "successful" career may be an important medium through which middle class men seek to establish masculine identities in the workplace. . . . Committed to upward progress, men in organizations are willing to work longer hours, meet tight deadlines, travel extensively, participate in residential training courses and move house at the behest of the company. (Collinson & Hearn, 1996, p. 161)

Working long hours is one way in which managers can differentiate themselves from their colleagues. A manager explains how this works: "If you work seventy hours per week then it is assumed that you are not well organized; if you work only forty hours they say: 'Don't you have anything to do?'" Another sums up why many managers work so much: "They never say you have to work overtime but you have to do it to do a good job; I do not write overtime because I have to finish a task, however long it takes" (Knoppers & Anthonissen, 2004). Many managers claim that their work is like a hobby. They acknowledge that they often do not have to work so many hours but say that they love what they do. Hatcher (2003) argues that showing such passion for their job is a relatively new requirement for managers. They always have had to sell themselves as being heroic and rational, but now they have to present themselves as passionate for the organization. Heroism and passion are seen as synonymous with commitment. This heroic passion may mask and justify excessive numbers of hours on the job. Thus, the institutionalization of passion helps to justify the priority placed on work over home responsibilities.

Although passion for the job may energize managers to work many hours, they also need stamina and ways to reduce the stress that accompanies their work. Sport involvement often plays a direct role in this. Being physically fit may enable managers to work long hours and to rarely call in sick (even when they are). Top-level managers often are proud of their ability to work even when sick. One senior manager exclaims: "I have worked here for four years and have not been absent one day; I get irritated with employees and colleagues who stay home with a headache!" (Knoppers & Anthonissen, 2004). Personal sport practices, ranging from being a member of a gym to playing basketball at the noon hour, are ways to handle stress and to build up the endurance that is needed to survive managerial work. Being able to work long hours differentiates the stronger managers from the weaker ones.[10]

Managers gain credibility when they distance themselves from poor health and from everyday domestic responsibilities. They are seen as being in control of themselves and their families. Such control is perceived to be an important asset in careerist discourses.[11] Managers with families are viewed more favorably than those without. Lyon and Woodward (2004) argue that a man who is seen as a family man is perceived to be trustworthy and reliable. Family men's relationships with the children and a wife may be distant, given the long hours away from home, but *having* a home indicates that they can manage personally as well as professionally. This aspect of careerist discourse is often incompatible with discourses about shared responsibility for domestic tasks and also tends to exclude many women and men to whom domestic caregiving is equally, if not more, important than their managerial work.

Interestingly, while a considerable amount of slippage tends to occur between work and home life, usually work intrudes into home life rather than the other way around. Senior managers tend to talk little about their home situation at work, while they do talk about their work at home. At work, home remains invisible. Top managers usually do not construct their work as a place to share home life, while home is seen as a place to express frustration and anger at events in the workplace. A senior manager describes how careful he has to be when talking about home life at work. He says: "Some managers do talk with a few specific others about their home life but are very careful about whom they do it with." This comment by another manager illustrates the gendered nature of this disconnect between work and home. He says: "I talk about such things only with my secretary [who is female]" (Knoppers & Anthonissen, 2004). This discourse, therefore, contradicts the informalist discourse that allows for intimate sharing among men. Sharing emotional intimacies between men may be limited. He rarely describes doubts about a son who does not date, amazement at a daughter who is obsessed with boys, or an intent to be more loving toward his wife. Obviously the degree of emotional sharing has boundaries as well. As long as individuals continue to seek individual solutions to cope with the demands of careers, little structural change will occur in the demands made by "hungry" institutions and the definitions of desirable masculinities which work in them.

A competitive sport background may facilitate careerism not only indirectly, in relieving stress and building stamina, but also directly (Collinson & Hearn, 1996). Research shows that a history of having played competitive sports in high school and university exerts an influence in the selection process for managers in areas ranging from the military to sport to the ministry to investment banking (Barrett, 1996; Jones, 1998). The values assigned to sport participation depend on social class, thus adding a layer of complexity to the situation (Coakley, 2007). For men in lower social classes, development of team and/or personal discipline and obedience (often stimulated by authoritarian practices) receive greater emphasis. For men from higher social classes, leadership skills and perseverance (careerism) tend to be emphasized. One manager with a competitive sport background says: "In sport you learn how to achieve and produce results." Another says: "[In sport] you develop persistence and endurance" (Knoppers & Anthonissen, 2004).

As the opening chapters have shown, men often create ways of doing masculinity in which they can distinguish themselves from each other and be united in differentiating themselves from that which they associate with women and gays. Often this occurs in competitive ways. Maier & Messerschmidt (1998), for example, find that commonalities and differences in the masculinities constructed by managers and engineers played a role in the *Challenger* disaster of 1986. The competition between managers and engineers disrupted their ability to work as a functional, effective team. Consequently, they missed key flaws in the construction and launch of the *Challenger*, contributing to the disaster of its explosion. This competitiveness among men in the workplace suggests that Taylor's recommendation that sport habits (baseball) become part of managerial discursive practices seems to be partially fulfilled, sometimes in deeply dysfunctional ways.

The degree to which a sport background enhances careerism depends to some extent on meanings given to the body and physicality in the primary activity of an organization (Knoppers, 2009). In organizations where physical strength is assigned an important role in intimidation and dominance such as in public safety and the armed forces, a sport background and an appearance of physical strength is judged to be a greater asset than one in which the primary activity of the organization centers on caring for the body such as in health care (Knoppers, 2009). Managers who worked in the health care sector said little about physicality while those who worked for the police often mentioned physicality without being asked about it specifically. One senior police manager says, "even the way you walk says something about your style of leadership and what you think is important"; another, "At the academy we learned more about sport than we did about management" (Knoppers & Anthonissen, 2004). Compensation for a lack of physicality occurs, however, when certain forms of managerial masculinity that are allied with organizational power and technical-professional domination, such as senior or partnership status, allow men to dominate without being physically strong (Cheng, 1999). Their status gives such men the power that they need.

The particular ways in which male managers refer to and rely on sport and physicality in entrepreneurial, informalist, and careerist discursive practices rely on context. Social class, type of work, and the nature of the organization all play a role. However, in most circumstances, being involved in sport—either through watching or playing—benefits male over female managers.

PARADOXES AND COMPLEXITIES

Meanings given to sport and managerial practices, and their relationships, vary more than the above discussion may suggest. Managers tend to draw from their repertoire of discourses, pulling out whichever one works best in a given situation, sometimes leading to paradoxes (Padavic & Earnest, 1994). Discursive practices not only overlap with each other but also change in relation to their context. Many discourses about athletic and managerial masculinities, for example, emphasize being in control, functioning as discourses of dominance. Yet, neither athletes nor managers and leaders are always in control. They, too, must conform at times, depend on others, and subordinate themselves. Although they influence organizational culture, senior managers answer to others, such as the director, the chief executive officer, chair of the board, owners, and so forth. At these times, they behave as a subordinate, following the wishes of others, putting others and/or team first, acting in a deferential manner, and so on.[12] Thus, senior managers play at least two roles, sometimes dominating, sometimes subordinating themselves.

In a further paradox, they enact both dependence and independence. Managers often emphasize that one of the aspects that they enjoy the most in their job is their independence (Knoppers, 2009). According to one manager, a person is responsible for his or her own success. However, the truth of the matter is that managers and leaders cannot remain completely independent; they depend on their subordinates, colleagues, and even volunteers for pertinent information, for reaching organizational goals, and for being judged as successful. Thus, their independence is limited. Ironically, though, their dependencies are rarely mentioned in managerial discourses.

A contributing factor to the complexity of these discourses is the adversarial nature of interpersonal professional relationships. Just as sport discourses require athletes to achieve individual excellence, while simultaneously subordinating their interests to the team's, so, too, informalism requires homosociality (a social preference for the company of men), while careerism requires heterosexuality (a sexual preference for women) (Kiesling, 2005). Further, while careerism requires differentiation, entrepreneurialism requires cultural cloning (Essed, 2002). Paradoxes run through all professional sets of discourses.

Complexity is evident in other ways as well. Social relations such as gender, social class, ethnicity, race, and sexuality are created simultaneously through discourse (Acker, 2000). Therefore, discourses by and about managers are not just limited to gender but also affect other social forces such as social class and race. As indicated earlier, not all forms of masculinity fit managerial discourses (Billing & Alvesson, 1994). Some managerial discourses are more congruent with discourses of middle- to upper-class masculinities than with working-class masculinities.

Further, the impact of sport on various discursive practices may be less straightforward than it seems. Although dominant managerial discourses and practices are primarily those created by white managers, little is known about how these discourses are influenced by dominant meanings given to images of black athletes and, therefore, how they would affect the actions of white or black managers. As an earlier chapter indicates, the media often represent black athletes differently than they do white male athletes. These meanings may influence the perceived suitability of athletes for senior-level managerial work. Black managers may be associated with sport in a negative sense, meaning that their managerial competency would be questioned, given the stereotype that sport is the only activity they can do well.[13] With the exception of a few black top athletic stars, a sport background may yield few collective advantages for blacks (Coakley, 2007). In addition, not all white employees or directors might accept entrepreneurial discursive practices from either black men or white or black women. Assertive black managers may be judged differently from assertive white managers by their white employees. Thus, the use of these dominant managerial discursive practices is influenced by meanings given to gender, class, race, ethnicity, sexuality, and other social group relations.

Meanings given to the primary activity of an organization also create complexities in the meanings given to managerial discourses. Acker (1992) notes this connection. Certain activities such as nursing or teaching, for example, are more associated with women, while firefighting or policing may be associated more with men. The use of gendered logic affects the meanings of managerial work in these organizations. For example, in health care organizations, the primary activity consists of caring for human bodies. Employees must be physically and emotionally strong in various ways to help clients. Similarly, members of the police and the military must be physically and emotionally strong to enable them to perform their duties in forceful and often dominating ways (Ott, 1989). These strengths are judged differently. Some are thought to be more appropriate for women and others more for men. These differences may influence the depth of meaning that physicality and sport hold in managerial discourses and practices. Managers in police organizations may tend to honor athletic masculinities differently than those in health care organizations. Thus, the salience of gendered discourses about athleticism in relation to managerial work may differ depending on the primary activity of the organization.

REFLECTIONS

Sport and meanings given to it fan out into society and culture. Using management as an example, this chapter analyzes the ways in which discourses about sport, masculinity, and management overlap and reinforce each other. Managerial discourses may intersect and support meanings given to athletic masculinities and vice versa. They allow men to differentiate themselves from all that is associated with femininities. Masculinities are continually challenged and reshaped, yet always in the context of not being associated with womanly things. In professional life, men who are portrayed as caring fathers or as people-oriented managers take pains to be seen as men who are confident of their own masculinity rather than as men who are associated with a type of femininity. Men who work in organizations associated with women (such as nursing or teaching) work hard to create masculinities that differentiate them from femininities (Dellinger, 2004).

Advocating for and bringing about change in the ways management at the senior level is conducted and constructed is complex, in part because it requires changes at the individual, collective, and organizational levels. In the introduction of this book we cited various caring actions by individuals and institutions/organizations whose net result is greater humanity for all people. How could they be applied to the management of organizations? First, change at the individual level requires managers to be aware that they are part of a socially constructed system in which (their) power plays a large role. This realization and consciousness of their own power as well as of the literally man-made nature of managerial work could for example give managers more room to be creative and innovative rather than assuming they have to be cultural clones of other senior managers or that they work in gender neutral ways. In addition, as P. Y. Martin (2003) points out, gender is often practiced in organizations in liminal ways, that is, many may not be aware they are engaging in it in ways that exclude or diminish the full humanity of others. This is especially true of senior managers/directors.

This chapter gives many examples of how that may occur. Change therefore requires a willingness to reflect on one's own practices accompanied by the assumption that they are gendered and by willingness to change when those practices exclude or denigrate. Senior managers occupy positions of power and therefore have a degree of freedom to act in ways that reflect an ethic of care and can influence others/their peers. They can set an example for individual relationships/interactions within an organization by, for example, stressing the need for an ethic of care and embodying such an ethic in their decision and policy making, and ways of interacting and leading. In addition, they can reward and value the often invisible care work that occurs in organizations, often done by women. Such reflexivity means they are sensitive not only to what they as an individual can do to make organizations more caring but also to the effect of their collective practices, i.e. male solidarity that mobilizes masculinities (Martin, 2003).

Leaders can ask themselves the following questions: Which ways of doing femininity and masculinity tend to be excluded by the use of dominant managerial discourses and/or are not included in these discursive practices as described in this chapter? To what extent is there room for alternate discourses? Are such spaces only created when tied to specific people such as Bill Gates and Dennis Rodman, who have been defined as being successful? How is organizational culture created and managed by men doing and thinking masculinity and how are they influenced by sport talk, by images of athletic masculinities, and by sport practices?

Change may be difficult but not impossible. The fact that there is an overlap between management and sport discourses means that changing discourses in sport may change managerial discourses and vice versa. Think how different the images and discourses related to management and sport would be if discourses that emphasized raising children, recreational walking, family games, joint caring for children's welfare, and a responsibility for the welfare of others dominated work life.

NOTES

1. The shape of management was not only influenced by sport; other social forces such as the growth of Protestantism (the Protestant work ethic) and of capitalism played a role. It is beyond the scope of this chapter to tease out the nature of the confluence, because the focus is on the interactions between meanings given to physicality or sport and management.

2. The job of managing a household, however, was not seen as managerial work.

3. For a discussion of this, see for example, Collinson & Hearn, 1996; Hall, Cullen, & Slack, 1990; Hearn, 1998; Wajcman, 1998.

4. See for example, the book edited by Davidson & Burke, 2004; Hall, Cullen, & Slack, 1990; Theberge, 2003.

5. See for example, Meyerson & Kolb, 2000; Shaw & Slack, 2002; www .theglassceiling.com.

6. The critical research in management has developed a body of literature focusing on managerial men as men, that is, the degree to which various forms of masculinity shape and dominate processes of organizing, and, how managers do and think gender; see for example, Collinson & Hearn, 1996; Kerfoot & Knights, 1998; Kvande 2002.

7. The others discussed by Collinson & Hearn are authoritarianism ("I am the boss; you have to do what I say!") and paternalism ("Let's discuss it but I know what is best for you").

8. This time factor also plays a role in another discourse (careerism) and will be discussed there.

9. The structure and organization of Promise Keepers, an association of Christian men, provides an interesting example of this use of sport as a place for emotional bonding among males.

10. Often the time taken to play tennis or basketball or to work out is also time away from family/domestic responsibilities. This means that a fifty-hour week may become a sixty-hour week.

11. This discourse is also often used to account for the scarcity of women managers. Women's domestic arrangements are assumed to get in the way of doing outstanding work because the structure of management still assumes, as it did in the early 1900s, that there is a support person at home. This assumption is rarely questioned by business executives or senior leaders and may explain in part why relatively few women in top functions in and outside of sport are single and/or do not have children (McKay, 1997).

12. See Maier, 1999, for a discussion of this point.

13. See for example, Hartmann, 2000; Jarvie & Reid, 1997; Johnson & Roediger, 2000; McGinn, D. (2005).

CONCLUSION

Human Being: Degendering Life

> Clearly, in common parlance, the phrase 'doing gender'
> evokes conformity; "undoing gender" evokes resistance
> (Deutsch, 2007).

Even though a pregnant woman feels her baby's physicality quite long before birth, a human body's physicality first becomes visible when it is born. After babies are born, we can see them move, kick, roll over, crawl, and eventually stand and walk and run. All those baby actions are ascribed meaning, often related to her or his perceived gender. "Oh, what a strong little man!" Aunt Nancy might exclaim. Uncle Joel might crow, "What a graceful little girl Katie is!" So "natural" does this feel that we do not even think about the fact that Aunt Nancy's words treat a baby like a future man and Uncle Joel's frame a baby as a little girl. Already, the words carve out future possibilities and limits for these tiny human beings. The meanings our gender-biased language gives to those babies' actions fall on a continuum with those given to actions of adults. Whether directed at babies or not, perceptions of gender-appropriate actions and behaviors lie deeply embedded in societal structures, such as language, and find reflection and force in collective cultural practices.

In this book, we have explored ways in which people impose gendered meanings, with or without good reason, on physically active bodies. These meanings reflect a given culture's deeply held assumptions about masculinities and femininities; more often than not, contradictions, paradoxes, and taboos lurk within those deep structures.

Dominant discourses about the human body as it gives birth, relates to others through touch, engages in sport, and manages the activities of others overlap in ways that operate according to hidden subtexts which may systematically harm, devalue, and/or exclude women or men. As authors we cannot only show how gender has been done in these areas; in this chapter we present possibilities for change, ways to 'undo gender.' For us, undoing gender, or degendering, depends upon an ethic of care because such an ethic places responsibility not only on individuals, but also on groups, institutions, organizations, and cultures to bring about change that serves the good of everyone who lives in them. In this case, an ethic of care calls for working toward situations of gender equity and justice, situations in which women and men of all sorts can flourish.

DEGENDERING

Gendering occurs everywhere people's actions are policed for gender-appropriate actions. Every time a birthing mother is told to let doctors decide what should be done to her during her labor, gendering occurs. Every time a set of parents is ridiculed for cosleeping with their children on the grounds of the sexual rights of the father, gendering has happened. Gendering occurs whenever a woman is told she should not attempt a high ski jump because of her gender. Whenever a man is told he should be interested in football, even when he is not, gendering occurs. If a woman is excluded from pay raises because she was not able to join in with the men on their sporting outings and is seen as not quite fitting in, again, gendering has occurred.

Feminist theorist F. M. Deutsch (2007) distinguishes between "doing gender" and "undoing gender." Doing gender means engaging in practices and discourses that strengthen hegemonically constructed differences. Undoing gender calls for resistant practices and discourses that weaken those deeply embedded meanings or suggest alternatives. For feminist theorist J. Lorber (2000), these actions of resisting or trying to undo mainstream gendering practices are best understood as "degendering." Neither the idea of "undoing gender" nor of "degendering" obliterates distinctions between women and men as persons but instead both emphasize the use or development of practices or discourses that do not devalue, harm, exclude, or categorize. More positively, "undoing gender" or "degendering" evokes ideas of equal regard, encouragement, inclusion, and imagination in relation to women and men of all types, and in relation to masculinities and femininities of all sorts.

Is change possible? Can alternative masculinities that oppose the norm of devaluing things associated with the "feminine" in all situations/contexts replace dominant forms that degrade? Can alternative femininities, that value and enact "womanly" be respected and become desirable and necessary in all areas of life? Can cultural spaces for people who do not fit categories of male or female neatly, such as transgendered and transsexual persons, be increased? We contend that all these are possible. Throughout this book, we have shown that even the most seemingly intransigent discourses are not totalizing. We have pointed out contradictions between dominant discourse and individual practices because these are just exactly the places where change can begin and can continue. Degendering, or undoing gender, can occur at various levels and can often be located in contradictions themselves.

UNGENDERING PHYSICALITY

In this book, we have explained how several interlocking systems of symbolically maintained power relations operate, from birth, to family life, to sport, to management. In each case, we presented people and actions that affected those relations, reshaping them, undoing the gendering within them. These points of resistance open doors to understanding how concern for the flourishing of common humanity rather than gender role appropriateness can lead to a vision of mutual care and responsibility for all people.

Giving birth, although obviously a highly physical female-specific activity, finds its meanings and subsequent protocols and practices given shape and substance by men as well as women, sometimes even more by men than by women. As chapter 1 shows, dominant discourses about childbirth practices are continually being negotiated in the United States. On the one hand, the mainstream medical profession maintains entrenched control over hospital-based protocols and procedures. Stories of women's strength in the face of pressures to conform show personal resistance, such as the story of Sandra, the woman whose birthing was managed impersonally by her doctors, who had appendicitis after giving birth and who advocated for herself until she found a doctor who listened to her, shows ways gender equity can come about. It takes tenacity and trusting one's knowledge of one's own body and listening and deciding to act on the basis of someone's story rather than strict protocols on the part of institutional caregivers. Other stories in *The Birthing Archive* tell equally direct tales of how women sought out caregivers who listened to them and took their telling into account. Some created lay midwife training groups; some used only midwives and birthing centers; some maintained their right to choose vaginal birthing when their babies were in a breech position. Structurally and institutionally, alternative discourses, such as those giving presence and privilege to midwives, doulas, and husbands as partners in the process rather than observers, open up more choices for women. Home birth and birthing centers can become viable alternative birthing sites when institutions, as well as persons, pay attention to what would constitute more humane birthing practices.

Physically active bodies interact with each other in various ways, one of which is through touch. Just as with birthing, gendered meanings given to touch also have shifted over time, moving toward increasing human agency for women and children. Over time, discourses that granted men unquestioned access to bodies of children and women have been resisted, argued against, and changed. Resistant discourses that evolved into laws against rape, especially date rape and marital rape, and laws against sexual harassment in work situations are good examples of how women and children can be valued as individuals whose bodies belong to them. A more positive discourse is being heard that argues touching and being touched are crucial to human life and growth, whether one is young or older. However, as so often is the case, one that imposes sexuality on all kinds of touch often counters this positive humanity-affirming discourse. Due to the sexualizing of all touch, this definition encourages many well-meaning people from holding or even hugging people they love. That takes affectionate touch out of life, impoverishing people by its loss. In the face of such discourses, families may choose to do as they see best, snuggling with their children in a big family bed. In one family we know, since the grandmother buys into the mainstream story of cosleeping's dangers and implicit sexuality, the mom and dad keep furniture in their children's bedrooms to give the semblance of decorum for grandma (and in readiness for the day when their children take to their own beds) and continue to do what suits them. In doing so, they enrich their own and their children's lives.

Sport's social domain, whose physical activities are enjoyed by both women and men, is filled with gendered meanings given to practices of physically active bodies. Initially, discourses about modern sport did not even imagine women as participants, and certainly not in competitive situations. Instead, only men were named as qualified participants; competitiveness was framed as "masculine;" and sport in general was associated primarily with the kinds of masculinities ascribed to 'the Christian gentleman' and Muscular Christianity. Over time, however, equity-affirming change has driven actors, actions, and discourses in sport. Women have entered competitively into all areas of sport, as their successes in all sports, up to and including extreme sports such as windsurfing and snowboarding, attest. Consequently, many discourses about sport have shifted to include all human beings and a wide diversity of sports and masculinities and femininities.

While much has changed, sport remains a place where some femininities and effeminacy can be devalued with impunity. Even though such practices continue, resistance meets gendering practice with ungendering practice. Every time new sport forms are created and celebrated, when coed participation grows, when pioneers become the first black or white woman or man to participate in a specific sport, when elite athletes come out of the closet, when transgendered athletes compete without being questioned, and when every human being is urged to be physically active for their good health, sports' playing field becomes more welcoming to human beings. Rather than the use of culturally inflected language that enforces the gender policing of "femininity" and "masculinity," "push back" acts and practices will continue to revolutionize how we talk about physically active bodies, until finally we reach a day when the emphasis is more on what healthy physically active bodies can do rather than what they look like and if that fits one's gender.

Many people are physically active in the world of paid work; here, as well as in so many other places, gendered meanings overlay actions. Especially senior, or upper, management still excludes women and also men of subordinated masculinities, often by celebrating sport-related practices of masculinity. The kind of men who discursively manage in entrepreneurial, informal, and careerist ways and who ally themselves with metaphors and practices from the world of professional men's sport experience the most advantages from dominant sport discourses. Senior management tends to be the places where decisions are made that influence an entire organization at every level, from the individual to the structural and symbolic levels. Often when powerful men transgress dominant versions of masculinity, their actions continue to be framed in terms of masculinity, such as "heroism" or physical and moral "strength," instead of in terms of performing practices related to femininity. We showed how senior male managers pride themselves on their people skills but do not see the use of those skills as a practice typically associated with femininity. The conflation of power and masculinity in public contexts, such as business, law, and government, may be one of the most intransigent social and organizational forces to resist, let alone change.

Our analysis of managerial discourses also showed a shift, however, from an emphasis on highly gendered mechanistic styles to ones that emphasize the use of human relational perspectives, points of view that engender by positively incorporating "womanly" qualities into what is considered exemplary managerial practice. Many women have been able to seize on this new discourse as warrant for their entry into and promotion within middle- and upper-middle management, into areas where "people skills" are considered mandatory. In this case, shifts in required managerial competencies line up with recognition that women brought about necessary changes in managerial work. Consequently, management is seen as an arena where women and men both work, rather than just being a "men's only" club. As women make their ways into the uppermost reaches of institutions, such as government, women such as Hillary Clinton, Sonia Sotomayor, and Angela Merkel are making a difference in how institutional work may be done. Through persons such as these and new institutional and cultural practices, change (slowly) takes place.

Changes give evidence of the strength of the human spirit. People are not robots who act out their socialization. Instead, they live as thinking and reflective persons. So, we conclude that neither men nor women *individually* are the problem when it comes to "doing gender," but *collectively*, the meanings given to masculinity and femininity are, especially, meanings that indicate women are worth less than men. Differences in valuation permeate people's sense of their own gender identity, their interactions, meanings they ascribe to other people, events, and even ideas. Devaluation does not require our recognition of it in order for it to happen. Gender theorist P. Y. Martin (2003) calls practices in which we "do gender" unaware "unreflexive practice." When people just "do gender" as they have learned it, unfair or hurtful talk and practices maintain the status quo.

A wider range of possibilities and behaviors is opened up to people when they reflect on their own practices and are not constrained by the artificial (but effective) barriers of paradox and taboo. As we have argued throughout this book, gender paradoxes and taboos work together to reduce humanity itself. If change is to occur, individuals and institutions need to prioritize the creation of discourses that point to human healing and wholeness, to discourses that undo gender. We believe that re-formation can occur leading to fuller life for all people if there is an individual and collective willingness to engage in this transformation and to understand the paradoxes and taboos of gendered meanings as they affect the ways we give meaning to physicality. This calls for a transcendent frame of reference, transcendent in the sense that dominant discourses about masculinities and femininities in the public sphere are questioned and alternatives tried and developed. Human discourses on gender are not fixed blueprints that follow genetic necessity but instead are social constructions that can be changed. Discourses that subordinate and marginalize need to be identified and defined and subsequently redefined and disrupted to allow people to be in mutuality- and equity-based relationship with each other, creating communities of love and care, instead of perpetuating (even if unintentionally) gendered hierarchies of values. We challenge ourselves and readers to create positive discourses in the place of harmful ones, to find and promote discourses that value the humanity of all that is "womanly," regardless of who shows that behavior.

In part, answers to "why?" practices and meanings are the way they are goes right along with formulating answers for "how?" change can come about. Stimulating perceived need for change and then implementing it may come from placing discourses in a countercultural, cross cultural, and/or historical perspective and from exposing contradictions as we have tried to do in this book. These already suggest alternatives.

LIVING OUT THE UNDOING OF GENDER

To describe ways to create new ways of speaking and living is difficult. We, whether authors or readers, all are influenced by the world in which we live. We do not have a magic solution that will undo all the gendering in this world. Our analysis already gives many insights and therefore ideas for possible alternatives. We can suggest several other possibilities. Our goals echo those of philosopher Nicholas Wolterstorff who calls people to work together for a day when justice and peace embrace (Wolterstorff, 1983). To us this means seeking to show respect and care for each other, calling each other to account when we fail, supporting each other when we try, and encouraging one another toward success in valuing all persons and a wide range of gender behaviors, no matter who enacts them. Focusing on these actions leads to undoing gender.

We can start simply by questioning "gendering" that is presented as common sense. Doing so calls for assuming that nothing is as it seems and that despite good intentions, people still can do harm. This discernment, seeing under the surface, is part of normal feminist consciousness. Ask yourself how you, whether intentionally or not, devalue behaviors, actions, or practices associated with "womanly" and elevate meanings associated with a certain form of masculinity in your everyday lives and how you talk to and about people. To what extent do you invest in the dominant and dominating discourses that demean, exclude, or denigrate a group of people, thereby making it more difficult for people to live their lives fully?

Working with and recognizing contradictions, paradoxes, and oppressive subtexts requires the development of an educated intuition, a discerning attitude toward 'common sense,' and a realization that as human beings we continually create and re-create meanings. These meanings are social constructions and therefore, what can be made can be changed and unmade.

Individual and Interaction Level

Change needs to transform interactions between people. Not only personal attitudes and decisions, but also interpersonal interactions build up the nature and character of gendered discourses, and therefore, hold potential for degendering. Meanings and their values are created through interactions (Weick, 1995). If interactions are to lead to change, planning and willingness to learn and change are required. Each of us needs to be aware of discourses that denigrate and be ready to call others on their negative actions toward others. In doing so, dominant meanings can be re-created. Lorber (2000) suggests that "whenever we can, we should encourage the degendering of instrumental tasks, physical labor, athletic prowess, emotional sustenance and physical spaces.

Every time a man changes a baby's diapers, it's a small rebellion; if he can do it in a gender-neutral public baby station, it's a social transformation" (p. 88). Similarly, men who wish to effect change need to reflect on how they mobilize masculinities to marginalize others when they are with other men. They need to explore how they privilege their own ways of seeing as "common sense," trivialize those men and boys who are seen as acting in "womanly" ways, and denigrate women in subtle ways (see Bird 1996; Martin, 2003, 2006 for more examples).

Dominant meanings can also be changed when women enact leadership in non-hegemonically masculine ways. Although women in positions of leadership often feel forced to do gender in stereotypic male ways, Deutsch (2007) suggests "exposure [of men and women] to women in leadership positions may decrease the difference in how competent and assertive men and women are perceived to be, despite the feminine performance of the leadership role" (p. 115).

Women and also men who are part of subordinated or marginalized masculinities need allies. Men with privilege and in high positions who love and care for people, no matter what sort of person they may be, can change the world through their speech and actions of support. A meaningful example of just this sort of alliance was enacted when Barack Obama, president of the United States, stood next to Lilly Ledbetter, early in 2009, at the signing of the Lilly Ledbetter Fair Pay Act. This civil rights act for women ensured that women could sue for equal pay for equal work, even years after the inequity first occurred. This was the first law President Obama signed. By choosing this as the first law to be signed and by choosing to have Lilly Ledbetter witness this act, President Obama sent a powerful signal about his respect for women in general and this woman in particular. This action by President Obama is also highly symbolic and illustrates how individual and symbolic levels are related. During our interactions we engage in sense making that influences how we visibly do and undo gender. At times these meanings have become embedded in structures and therefore need to be undone.

Structural Level

Change also has to occur in the systematic divisions within the world, intersecting with the activities that we associate with a particular group. J. Lorber calls for us to blur gender boundaries in our everyday lives and undermine the built-in gender divisions in our work worlds.

Although the focus of this book is not so much on the ways gender is embedded in policies and laws and in structures of society but on meanings given to behavior, actions, and practices, we do offer a few suggestions here as well since our hope is that emancipatory meanings become embedded in these structures. The breaking down or blurring of gender segregation in the public sphere has been implemented in many national, local, and institutional policies such as neighborhood provisions for child care, such as parental leave that assumes that all parents and not just mothers need it, such as the creation of an organizational climate with no tolerance for sexual harassment, such as the establishment of clearly defined organizational procedures for promotion and for salaries, and such as the use of comparable worth procedures to set salaries.

It is easy to confine undoing gender to structural change since that seems easier and does not require personal change. Such a limited focus has its drawbacks however. Connell (2006) points out an unexpected side effect of the implementation of such policies. She has shown how the presence of such policies is associated with a discourse of gender neutrality. Individuals assume no further degendering needs to occur. Consequently few individuals dare mention subtle gendered practices and meanings. We contend that structural change and implementation of humane and people-friendly policies do not exempt individuals from responsibility for degendering practices and meanings.

Symbolic Level

Despite individual acts of resistance, changes at the collective level thus far tend to represent more a modernization of certain practices of masculinities than a transformation of the values assigned to behaviors and practices associated with masculinities and femininities. Undoing gender requires naming and exposing the underlying discourses and the contradictions, disjunctures, and power conflicts. Symbolic change can come about by focused collective action (Connell, 1987; Lorber, 1994). People who are well-placed to move, to shift, to transform the very symbol systems that create and sustain hegemonic gendered meanings include all who serve as agents of symbolic control such as teachers, clergy, managers, and media makers. These are exactly the people who can produce alternatives, suggest new language, or engage in counter practices. Just through example, they can lead in degendering by undoing gender in the ways they speak and act. The story about President Obama cited earlier illustrates this well.

Overlapping discourses can also provide impetus for change. A change in discourses in one area of life materially will affect discourses in another area. For example, degendering discourses about sport may spill over into managerial discourses, thereby changing them as well. While some changes will raise the value of "womanly," others may question matters such as the routine and unthinking conflation of sexuality and gender.

REFLECTIONS

The individual, interactional, symbolic, and structural levels all intersect and influence each other. It is not enough to teach individuals not to be prejudiced, not to categorize, or not to hate or denigrate (although surely that is a beginning), but more importantly, awareness of the positive actions of degendering as acts of social justice also must play a role to ensure they become embedded in laws and policies and in discursive practices.

The more we focus proactively on undoing gender at all levels, not just noting the injustices done in the name of gender, the greater the possibility that dominant discourses of differentiation and (de) valuation will not only shift, but become undone. The more we engage in creating a world in which distinctions between male and female are limited to reproductive differences and not generalized into all of life, the less gender will organize culture, religion, and identities. What will be the result? Along with J. Lorber (2000) we argue:

> [I]n actuality, the modern world is both formal in organization and informal in practice, rule-based and relational, rational and emotional at one and the same time, and so are the people in it, women and men. Diminishment of gender as an organizing principle of institutions and everyday life would not turn women into men any more than it would turn men into women. It would rather degenderize the best—and the worst—qualities of people. (p. 90)

What would emerge would be a world of peace and justice in gender relations, a world in which human beings would flourish in all the varied ways they could imagine, plan, and live out.

Would the paradoxes and taboos disappear? No, many of them would remain, but perhaps fewer, and with less tenacity. More spaces would open up for people to make their own graceful contributions to life. We invite you to join in the contributions as you live out your life, both physically and within symbol systems, in families, with friends, as you play or watch sports and engage in physical activity, and as you carry out your paid and unpaid work in the world.

REFERENCES

Acker, J. (1992). Gendering organizational theory. In A. J. Mills & P. Tancred (Eds.), *Gendering organizational analysis* (pp. 248–262). Newbury Park, CA: Sage Publications.

Acker, J. (2000). Revisiting class: Thinking from gender, race, and organizations. *Social Politics, 7,* 192–214.

Acosta, V. R., & Carpenter, L. (2008). Women in intercollegiate sport: A longitudinal national study: Thirty-one year update, 1977–2008. Retrieved on November 15, 2008, from www.acostacarpenter.org.

Agar, J. (2004). "He's still our son in our hearts." Couple agonizes as they sever ties with troubled, adopted 10 year old boy. *Grand Rapids Press.* Retrieved from www.mlive.com/news/grpress.index.ssf?/base/news-1/108938482277600.xml

Agnew, T., Gilmore, J., & Sullivan, P. (1997). *A multicultural perspective of breastfeeding in Canada.* Ottawa, ON: Minister of Health.

Albrecht, S. L., Clarke, L. L., Miller, M. K., & Farmer, F. L. (1996). Predictors of differential birth outcomes among Hispanic subgroups in the United States: The role of maternal risk characteristics and medical care. *Social Science Quarterly, 77,* 407–434.

American Association of University Women. (1995). *How schools shortchange girls: The AAUW Report: A study of major findings on girls and education.* New York: Marlowe and Company.

Anderson, E. (2000). *Trailblazing: The true story of America's first openly gay track coach.* Los Angeles: Alyson Books.

Anderson, G. C. (1995). Touch and the kangaroo care method. In T. M. Field (Ed.), *Touch in Early Development* (pp. 35–51). Mahwah, NJ: Lawrence Erlbaum Associates.

Anderson, K. (1999). Snowboarding: The construction of gender in an emerging sport. *Journal of Sport & Social Issues, 23,* 55–79.

Andrews, D. L. (1999). Contextualizing suburban soccer: Consumer culture, lifestyle differentiation, and suburban America. *Culture, Sport, Society, 2(3),* 31–53.

Aucott, S., Donohue, P. K., Atkins, E., et al. (2002). Neurodevelopmental care in the NICU. *Mental Retardation and Developmental Disabilities Research Reviews, 8,* 298–308.

Austin, J. L. (1975). *How to do things with words.* Cambridge: Harvard University Press.

Banet–Weiser, S. (1999). Hoop dreams: Professional basketball and the politics of race and gender. *Journal of Sport & Social Issues, 23,* 403–420.

Barrett, F. (1996). The organizational construction of hegemonic masculinity: The case of the U.S. Navy. *Gender, Work & Organization, 3,* 129–142.

Bartkowski, J. (2000). "Breaking walls, raising fences: Masculinity, intimacy, and accountability among the Promise Keepers." *Sociology of Religion 61,* 33-53.

Beal, B. (1996). Alternative masculinity and its effects on gender relations in the subculture of skateboarding. *Journal of Sport Behavior, 19,* 204–220.

Benefits of breastfeeding. (2008). Retrieved March 11, 2008, from www.4women .gov/breastfeeding/index.cfm?page=227

Benjamin, O., & Sullivan, O. (1996). The importance of difference: Conceptualizing increased flexibility in gender relations at home. *The Sociological Review, 44,* 225–251.

Billing, Y. D., & Alvesson, M. (1994). *Gender, managers and organizations.* Berlin, Germany: De Gruyter.

Bird, S. (1996). Welcome to the men's club: Homosociality and the maintenance of hegemonic masculinity. *Gender & Society, 10,* 120–132.

Birdwhistell, R. L. (1970). *Kinesics and context.* Philadelphia: University of Pennsylvania Press.

Bohm, D. (1996). *On dialogue.* New York: Routledge.

Bravo, E. (2003, November 14). Wage gap persists between men, women. *Miami Herald.* Retrieved March 23, 2004, from www.commondreams.org/viewsoc/1114–03.htm

Breastfeeding. (2005). *Health topics: University of Iowa health care.* Retrieved March 12, 2008, from www.uihealthcare.com/topics/newborncare/newb4801 .html

Brief history. (n.d.). Retrieved August 29, 2005, from www.ymca.net/about/ cont/history.htm

Burstyn, V. (1999). *The rites of men: Manhood, politics and the culture of sport.* Toronto: University of Toronto Press.

Butler, J. (1993). *Bodies that matter: On the discursive limits of 'sex.'* New York: Routledge.

Butler, J. (1999). *Gender trouble* (10th ed.). New York: Routledge.

REFERENCES

Cahn, S. (1994). *Coming on strong: Gender and sexuality in twentieth century women's sport.* New York: Free Press.

Canary, D., & Dindia, K. (2006). *Sex differences and similarities in communication: Critical essays and empirical investigations of sex and gender in interaction* (2nd ed.). New York: Routledge.

Carlton, T., Callister, L. C., & Stoneman, E. (2005). Decision-making in laboring women: Ethical issues for perinatal nurses. *Journal of Prenatal & Neonatal Nursing, 19,* 145–155.

Caudwell, J. (1999). Women's football in the United Kingdom: Theorizing gender and unpacking the butch lesbian image. *Journal of Sport & Social Issues, 23,* 390–402.

Caulfield, R. (2000). Beneficial effects of tactile stimulation on early development. *Early Childhood Education Journal, 27,* 255–257.

Cavanagh, S. & Sykes, H. (2006). Transsexual bodies at the Olympics: The International Olympic Committee's policy on transsexual athletes at the 2004 Athens Summer Games. *Body & Society, 12,* 75–102.

Cheng, C. (1999). Marginalized masculinities and hegemonic masculinity. *Journal of Men's Studies, 7,* 295–315.

Claringbould, I. (2008). Mind the gap: The layered reconstruction of gender in sport-related organizations. Den Bosch/Nieuwegein; Mulier Instituut/Arko Sports Media.

Claringbould, I., & Elling, A. (2004). *Heldinnen in de sport. [Heroines in Sport].* Den Bosch/Nieuwegein; Mulier Instituut/Arko Sports Media.

Claringbould, I., & Knoppers, A. (2007). Finding a 'normal' woman: Selection processes for board membership. *Sex Roles, 56,* 495–507.

Claringbould, I., Knoppers, A., & Elling, A. (2004). Exclusionary practices in sport journalism. *Sex Roles, 51,* 709–718.

Clinton, W. J. (2004). *My life.* New York: Knopf.

Coakley, J. (2007). *Sport in society: Issues and controversies* (9th ed.). New York: McGraw-Hill.

Cohen, G. (1999). *American Academy of Pediatrics guide to your child's sleep.* New York: Villard Books.

Collinson, D. L., & Hearn, J. (1996). *Men as managers, managers as men: Critical perspectives on men, masculinities and managements.* London: Sage Publications.

Condry, S. M., Condry, J. C., & Pogatshnik, L. W. (1983). Sex differences: A study of the ear of the beholder. *Sex Roles, 9,* 697–704.

Connell, R. W. (1987). *Gender and power: Society, the person, and sexual politics.* Stanford, CA: Stanford University Press.

Connell, R. W. (2000). *The men and the boys.* Berkeley: University of California Press.

Connell, R. W. (2005). *Masculinities* (2nd ed.). Berkeley: University of California Press.

Connell, R. W. (2006) The experience of gender change in public sector organizations. *Gender, Work & Organization, 13*, 435–452.

The Council on Biblical Manhood and Womanhood. (2008). Retrieved March 10, 2008, from www.cbmw.org

Crosset, T., Benedict, J. R., & McDonald, M. A. (1995). Male student-athletes reported for sexual assault: A survey of campus police departments and judicial affairs offices. *Journal of Sport & Social Issues, 19*, 126–140.

Curry, T. (1998). Beyond the locker room: Campus bars and college athletes. *Sociology of Sport Journal, 15*, 205–215.

Cytotec: Drug description. (n.d.). Retrieved September 1, 2008, from www .rxlist.com/cgi/generic/misopro.htm

Dana S. (1996). Interview with Helen Sterk. *The Birthing Project Archive*. Milwaukee, WI: Marquette University Library.

Davidson, M., & Burke, R. (Eds.). (2004). *Women in management worldwide: Facts, figures, and analysis*. Burlington, VT: Ashgate Publishing.

Davis, L. R. (1997). *The swimsuit issue and sport: Hegemonic masculinity in Sports Illustrated*. Albany: State University of New York Press.

Davis, L. R., & Harris, O. (1998). "Race" and ethnicity in U.S. sportmedia. In L. Wenner (Ed.), *Mediasport* (pp. 154–169). London: Routledge.

Davison, K. G. (2000). Boys' bodies in school: Physical education. *Journal of Men's Studies, 8*, 255–266.

Dellinger, K. (2004). Masculinities in "safe" and "embattled" organizations: Accounting for pornographic and feminist magazines. *Gender & Society, 18*, 545–566.

Demetriou, D. Z. (2001). Connell's concept of hegemonic masculinity: A critique. *Theory and Society, 30*, 337–361.

Derks, M. (1999). Hard gras: Sekse, identiteit en voetbal geschiedenis (Hard grass: Gender, identity and the history of soccer). *Tijdschrift voor Gender Studies, 2*, 5–15.

Deutsch, F. M. (2007). Undoing gender. *Gender & Society, 21*, 106–127.

Disch, L., & Kane, M. J. (2000). When a looker is really a bitch: Lisa Olson, sport and the heterosexual matrix. In S. Birrell & M. McDonald (Eds.), *Reading sport: Critical essays on power and representation* (pp. 108–143). Boston: Northeastern University Press.

Dolin, D. J., & Booth-Butterfield, M. (1993). Reach out and touch someone: Analysis of nonverbal comforting responses. *Communication Quarterly, 14*, 383–393.

Duck, S. W. (1994). *Dynamics of relationships [Understanding relationship processes, 4]*. Thousand Oaks, CA: Sage Publication, 135–62.

Duncan, N. (1996). *Body space: Destabilizing geographies of gender and sexuality*. New York: Routledge.

Eldredge, J. (2001). *Wild at heart: Discovering the secret of a man's soul*. Nashville: Thomas Nelson.

Elling, A. (1999). Een beetje ruig, dat trekt me wel. Over het imago en de beleving van het vrouwenvoetbal ["A little rough, I like that": About the images of and experiences in women's soccer]. *Tijdschrift voor Genderstudies, 2*(4), 25–35.

Elling, A., de Knop, P., & Knoppers, A. (2003). Gay/lesbian sport clubs and events: Places of homo-social bonding and cultural resistance? *International Review for the Sociology of Sport, 38,* 441–456.

Emma V. (1996). Interview with Helen Sterk. *The Birthing Project Archive.* Milwaukee, WI: Marquette University Library.

Engler, A. J., Luddington-Hoe, S. M., Cusson R. M., et al. (2002). Kangaroo care: National survey of practice, knowledge, barriers and perceptions. *American Journal of Maternal/Child Nursing, 27,* 146–153.

Epidural anesthesia. (2008). American Pregnancy Association. Retrieved September 2, 2008, from www.americanpregnancy.org/labornbirth/epidural.html

Epstein, A. (2008). *The business of being born.* New York: Barranca Productions.

Essed, P. (2002). Cloning cultural homogeneity while talking diversity: Old wine in new bottles in Dutch organizations. *Transforming Anthropology, 11,* 2–12.

Feldman, R., Weller, A., Sirota, L., et al. (2002). Skin-to-skin contact (kangaroo care) promotes self-regulation in premature infants: Sleep-wake cyclicity, arousal modulation, and sustained exploration. *Developmental Psychology, 38,* 194–207.

Feldman, R., Weller, A., Sirota, L., et al. (2003). Testing a family intervention hypothesis: The contribution of mother-infant skin-to-skin contact (kangaroo care) to family interaction, proximity and touch. *Journal of Family Psychology, 17,* 94–107.

Ferber, R. (1986). *Solve your child's sleep problems.* New York: Fireside.

Field, C. (Producer and director). (1999). *The life and times of Rosie the riveter* [Motion picture]. Santa Monica, CA: Direct Cinema Limited.

Flanagan, C. (2004). How serfdom saved the women's movement. *The Atlantic Monthly.* Retrieved May 5, 2004, from www.theatlantic.com/issues/2004/03/flanagan.htm

Floyd, K., & Morman, M. T. (2000). Reacting to the verbal expression of affection in same sex interaction. *Southern Communication Journal, 65,* 94–107.

Foucault, M. (1977). *Discipline and punish: The birth of the prison.* New York: Pantheon Books.

Friedan, B. (1963). *The feminine mystique.* New York: Norton.

Fuentes-Afflick, E., Hessol, N. A., & Perez-Stable, E. (1999). Testing the epidemiological paradox of low birth weight in Latinos. *Archives of Pediatrics & Adolescent Medicine, 153,* 147–148.

Gerber, E. W. (1974). *The American woman in sport.* Reading, MA: Addison-Wesley.

Giulianotti, R. (1999). *Football: A sociology of the global game.* Cambridge, U.K.: Polity Press.

Glantz, J. C. (2003). Labor induction rate variation in upstate New York: What is the difference? *Birth, 30,* 168–174.

Goebel, P. W. (2002). Fathers' touch in low birth weight infants. *Dissertation Abstracts International, 62.8B,* 3553.

Goer, H. (1995). *Obstetric myths versus research realities: A guide to the medical literature.* Westport, CT: Bergin & Garvey.

Gooren, J. (2008). Olympic sports and transsexuals. *Asian Journal of Andrology, 10,* 427–432.

Gould, J. B., Davey, B., & Stafford, R. S. (1989). Socioeconomic differences in rates of cesarean section. *The New England Journal of Medicine, 321,* 233–240.

Grey, J. (1993). *Men are from Mars, women are from Venus: A practical guide for improving communication and getting what you want in your relationships.* New York: HarperCollins.

Griffin, P. (1998). *Strong women: Deep closets.* Champaign, IL: Human Kinetics.

Gupta, M. A., & Schork, N. J. (1995). Touch deprivation has an adverse effect on body image: Some preliminary observations. *International Journal of Eating Disorders, 17,* 185–189.

Gurian, M. (1997). *The wonder of boys.* New York: J.P. Tarcher.

Gurian, M. (1999). *A fine young man: What parents, mentors and educators can do to shape adolescent boys into exceptional men.* New York: J. P. Tarcher.

Hall, M. A. (1996). *Feminism and sporting bodies: Essays on theory and practice.* Champaign, IL: Human Kinetics.

Hall, M. A., Cullen, D., & Slack, T. (1990). *The gender structure of national sport organizations. Sport Canada. Occasional papers, vol. 2.* Ottawa, ON: Government of Canada, Fitness and Amateur Sport.

Hall, R. E. (2001). The bell curve: Calculated racism and the stereotype of African American men. *Journal of Black Studies, 32,* 104–119.

Hargreaves, J. (1994). *Sporting females: Critical issues in the history and sociology of women's sports.* London: Routledge.

Hargreaves, J. (2000). *Heroines of Sport: The politics of difference and identity.* London: Routledge.

Harrison, C. K. (1998). Themes that thread through society: Racism and athletic manifestation in the African–American community. *Race, Ethnicity and Education, 1,* 63–74.

Harrison, C. K., & Lawrence, S. M. (2004). College students' perceptions, myths, and stereotypes about African-American athleticism: A qualitative investigation. *Sport, Education and Society, 9,* 33–52.

Hartmann, D. (2000). Rethinking the relationships between sport and race in American culture: Golden ghettos and contested terrain. *Sociology of Sport Journal, 3,* 229–253.

Hartmann, K., Viswanathan, M., & Palmieri, R. (2005). Outcomes of routine episiotomy: A systematic review. *Journal of the American Medical Association, 293*, 2141–2148.

Hatcher, C. (2003). Refashioning a passionate manager: Gender at work. *Gender, Work & Organization, 10*, 391–412.

Healthy pregnancy: C-Section by choice. (2006). WebMD. Retrieved August 13, 2008, from blogs.webmd.com/healthy-pregnancy/2006/010c-section-by -choice.html

Hearn, J. (1989). Reviewing men and masculinities—or mostly boys' own papers. *Theory, Culture and Society, 6*, 665–689.

Hearn, J. (1998). On Ambiguity, contradiction and paradox in gendered organizations. *Gender, Work & Organization, 5*, 1.

Heino, R. (2000). What is so punk about snowboarding? *Journal of Sport & Social Issues, 24*, 176–191.

Hekma, G. (1994). *Als ze maar niet provoceren. Discriminatie van homoseksuele mannen en lesbische vrouwen in de georganiseerde sport [As long as they do not provoke: Discrimination of gay men and lesbians in organized sport].* Amsterdam, Netherlands: Het Spinhuis.

Henry, J., & Comeaux, H. (1999). Gender egalitarianism in coed sport: A case study of American soccer. *International Review for the Sociology of Sport, 34*, 277–290.

Hovden, J. (2000). Heavyweight men and younger women? The gendering of selection processes in Norwegian sport organizations. *NORA, 8*, 17–32.

Jane F. (1996). Interview with Helen Sterk. *The Birthing Project Archive.* Milwaukee, WI: Marquette University Library.

Janssen, A., & Weeden, L. K. (Eds.). (1994). *Seven promises of a promise keeper.* Colorado Springs, CO: Focus on the Family.

Jarvie, G., & Reid, I. (1997). Race relations. Sociology of sport and the new politics of race and racism. *Leisure Studies, 16*, 211–219.

Johnson, L., & Roediger, D. (2000). "Hertz, don't it?" Becoming colorless and staying black in the crossover of O. J. Simpson. In S. Birrell & M. McDonald (Eds.), *Reading sport: Critical essays on power and representation* (pp. 40–73). Boston: Northeastern University Press.

Jones, A. (1998). (Re)producing gender cultures: Theorizing gender in investment banking recruitment. *Geoforum, 29*, 451–474.

Jones, S. E. (1986). Sex differences in touch communication. *Western Journal of Speech Communication, 50*, 227–241.

Kam, K. (2008). Why women don't nurse longer. Retrieved March 12, 2008, from www.parenting.com/article/Baby/Feeding/moms-right-to-breastfeed

Kanter, R. M. (1977). *Men and women of the corporation.* New York: Basic Books.

Karsten, L., & Pel, E. (2000). Skateboarders exploring urban public space: Ollies, obstacles and conflicts. *Journal of Housing and the Built Environment, 15*, 327–340.

Keeley, M. P., & Hart, A. J. (1994). Nonverbal behavior in dyadic interaction. In S. W. Duck (Ed.), *Dynamics of relationships [Understanding relationship processes,4]* (pp. 135–162). Thousand Oaks, CA: Sage Publication.

Kelley, D. E. (Writer), & D'Elia, B. (Director). (2008). *Boston legal* [Television series]. Los Angeles: American Broadcasting Company.

Kerfoot, D., & Knights, D. (1998). Managing masculinity in contemporary organizational life: A "man"agerial project. *Organization, 5,* 7–26.

Kiesling, S. F. (2003). Prestige, cultural models and other ways of thinking about underlying norms and gender. In J. Holmes & M. Meyerhoff (Eds.), *Handbook of language and gender* (pp. 509–527). Oxford, U.K.: Blackwell Publishing.

Kiesling, S. F. (2005). Homosociality in men's talk: Balancing and recreating cultural discourses of masculinity. *Language in Society, 34,* 695–726.

Klein, A. (1993). *Little big men. Bodybuilding subculture and gender construction.* Albany: State University of New York Press.

Knoppers, A. (1999). "Voorhoede van Ajax spelt meisjesvoetbal": Gender and Voetbal [Ajax offense plays girls' soccer:' Gender and soccer]. *Tijdschrift voor Genderstudies, 2,* 16–24.

Knoppers, A. (2009). Giving meaning to sport involvement in managerial work. *Gender, Work and Organization, 16.*

Knoppers, A., & Anthonissen, A. (2001). Meanings given to performance in Dutch sport organizations: Gender and racial subtexts. *Sociology of Sport Journal, 18,* 302–316.

Knoppers, A., & Anthonissen, A. (2003). Women's soccer in the United States and the Netherlands: Differences and similarities in regimes of inequalities. *Sociology of Sport Journal, 20,* 351–370.

Knoppers, A., & Anthonissen, A. (2004). 'This is crazy! What difference does masculinity make?' Paper presented at the annual conference of the North American Society for the Sociology of Sport, Tucson, AZ, November 1–4.

Knoppers, A., & Anthonissen, A. (2005). Male athletic and managerial masculinities: Congruencies in discursive practices. *Journal of Gender Studies, 13,* 123–135.

Knoppers, A., & Anthonissen, A. (2008). Gendered managerial discourses in sport organizations: Multiplicity and complexity. *Sex Roles, 58,* 93–103.

Knoppers, A. (2009). Giving meaning to sport involvement in managerial work. *Gender, Work & Organization, 16.* Early view. DOI: 10.1111/j.1468-0432.2009.00467.x

Knoppers, A., & Bouman, Y. (1996). *Trainers/coaches: Een kwestie van kwaliteit? [Trainers/coaches: A question of quality?].* Papendal, Arnhem, the Netherlands: NOCNSF.

Knoppers, A., & Bouman, Y. (1998). De trainer als cultuurdrager. [The trainer as a mirror and creator of culture.] In J. Steenbergen, A. Buisman, P. de

Knop, & J. Lucassen (Eds.), *Waarden en normen in de sport: Analyse en beleidsperspectief* (pp. 223–239). Houten: Bohn Stafleu Van Loghum.

Knoppers, A., & Elling, A. (2001). Sport and the media: Race and gender in the re-presentation of athletes and events. In J. Steenbergen, P. De Knop, & A. Elling (Eds.), *Values & norms in sport. Critical reflections on the position and meanings of sport in society* (pp. 281–300). Oxford, U.K.: Meyer & Meyer Sport.

KNVB [Koninklijke Nederlandse Voetbal Bond]. (1997). *Jubileum boek vrouwenvoetbal [Anniversary book of women's soccer].* Zeist: KNVB.

KNVB [Koninklijke Nederlandse Voetbal Bond]. (2007). Jaarverslag 2007. [yearly report 2007] Retrieved on November 15, 2008, from files.datawire .nl/uploads/images4IUUas8KE1JnNEzoPosydQ/Jaarverslag_KNVB_2007 -2008.pdf

Kolnes, L. (1995). Heterosexuality as an organizing principle in women's sport. *International Review for the Sociology of Sport, 30,* 61–77.

Kopay, D. (2001) (1977). *The David Kopay story.* Los Angeles: Advocate Books.

Kvande, E. (2002). Doing masculinities in organizational restructuring. *NORA– Nordic Journal of Feminist and Gender Research, 10,* 16–25.

Laberge, S., & Albert, M. (1999). Conceptions of masculinity and gender transgressions in sport among adolescent boys: Hegemony, contestation, and social class dynamics. *Men and Masculinities, 1,* 243–267.

Ladd, T., & Mathisen, J. (1999). *Muscular Christianity: Evangelical Protestants and the development of American sport.* Grand Rapids, MI: Baker Books.

Lamb, M. E., Frodi, A. M., Frodj, M., & Hwant, C. P. (1982). Characteristics of maternal and paternal behavior in traditional and nontraditional Swedish families. *International Journal of Behavioral Development, 5,* 131–141.

Lapchick, R. (2006). *The 2005 race and gender report card.* Orlando: The Institute for Diversity and Ethics in Sport (TIDES). College of Business Administration: University of Central Florida.

Leathers, D. G. (1976). *Nonverbal communication systems.* Boston: Allyn & Bacon.

Leathers, D. G. (1986). *Successful nonverbal communication: Principles and applications.* New York: Macmillan.

Lee H. (1996). Interview with Helen Sterk. *The Birthing Project Archive.* Milwaukee, WI: Marquette University Library.

Lenskij, H. (1986). *Out of bounds: Women, sport and sexuality.* Toronto: Women's Press.

Lerner, G. (1993). *The creation of feminist consciousness: From the middle ages to eighteen-seventy.* New York: Oxford University Press.

Longman, J. (2001). *The girls of summer: The U.S. women's soccer team and how it changed the world.* New York: HarperCollins.

Looy, H., & Bouma, H. (2005). The nature of gender: Gender identity in persons who are intersexed or transgendered. *Journal of Psychology and Theology, 33,* 166–178.

Lorber, J. (1994) *Paradoxes of Gender*. New Haven, CT: Yale.

Lorber, J. (2000). Using gender to undo gender: A feminist degendering movement. *Feminist Theory, 1*, 79–95.

Lorber, J. (2005). *Breaking the bowls: Degendering and feminist change*. New York: Norton.

Ludington-Hoe, S. (1993). *Kangaroo care: The best you can do to help your preterm infant*. New York: Bantam.

Lyon, D., & Woodward, A. (2004). Gender and time at the top: Cultural constructions of time in high level careers and homes. *European Journal of Women's Studies, 11*, 205–221.

Maier, M. (1999). On the gendered substructure of organization: Dimensions and dilemmas of corporate masculinity. In G. N. Powell (Ed.), *Handbook of Gender & Work* (pp. 69–93). London: Sage Publications.

Maier, M., & Messerschmidt, J. (1998). Commonalities, conflicts and contradictions in organizational masculinities: Exploring the gendered genesis of the Challenger disaster. *Canadian Review of Sociology and Anthropology, 35*, 325–344.

Marshall, P. (Director) & Greenhut, R. (Producer). (1992). *A league of their own* [Motion picture]. Los Angeles: Columbia Pictures Corporation.

Marson, G. M. (2000). Touch and the development of the body image disturbances among female college students. *Dissertation Abstracts International, 60*(11B), 5782.

Martin, K. A. (2003). Giving birth like a girl. *Gender & Society, 17*, 54–73.

Martin, P. Y. (2003). "Said and done" versus "saying and doing": Gendering practices, practicing gender at work. *Gender & Society, 17*, 342–366.

Martin, P. Y. (2006). Practising gender at work: Further thoughts on reflexivity. *Gender, Work & Organization, 13*, 254–276.

McDowell, L. (2001). Men, management and multiple masculinities in organizations. *Geoforum, 32*, 181–198.

McGinn, D. (2005). Jack on Jack: His next chapter. *Newsweek, 165*(145), nr. 14, 41–48.

McGinnis, M. (2004). Bed sharing is risky. *Prevention, 125*.

McGovern, P., Dowd, B., Gjerdingen, D., Gross, C. R., Kenney, S., Ukestad, L., et al. (2006). Postpartum health of employed mothers 5 weeks after childbirth. *Annals of Family Medicine, 4*, 159–167.

McKay, J. (1997). *MANaging gender*. Albany: State University of New York Press.

McKenna, J. J. (1996). Babies need their mothers beside them! *World Health, 49*(1), 14.

Mehrabian, A. (1981). *Silent messages: Implicit communication of emotion and attitudes* (2nd ed.). Belmont, CA: Wadsworth.

Mehus, I. (2005). Distinction through sport consumption: Spectators of soccer, basketball, and ski-jumping. *International Review for the Sociology of Sport, 40*, 321–333.

Messner, M. (1988). Sports and male domination: The female athlete as contested ideological terrain. *Sociology of Sport Journal, 5,* 197–211.

Messner, M. (1990). When bodies are weapons: Masculinity and violence in sport. *International Review for the Sociology of Sport, 25,* 203–220.

Messner, M. (1992). *Power at play.* Boston: Beacon Press.

Messner, M. (2002). *Taking the field: Women, men and sports.* Minneapolis: University of Minnesota Press.

Messner, M., & Sabo, D. (1994). *Sex, violence and power in sports: Rethinking masculinity.* Freedom, CA: Crossing Press.

Meyerson, D., & Kolb, D. (2000). Moving out of the armchair: Developing a framework to bridge the gap between feminist theory and practice. *Organization, 7,* 553–571.

Miller, C. A. (September/October 1987). A review of maternity care programs in western Europe. *Family Planning Perspectives, 19,* 207–211.

Miracle, M., & Rees, C. R. (1994). *Lessons of the locker room: The myth of school sports.* Amherst, NY: Prometheus Books.

Moodley, R. (1999). Masculine/managerial masks and the "other" subject. In S. Whitehead & R. Moodley (Eds.), *Transforming managers: Gendering change in the public sector* (pp. 214–233). London: UCL Press/Taylor & Francis.

National briefing science and health: Study on infant death syndrome. (2001, May 2). *The New York Times,* A16.

Nelson, M. B. (1994). *The stronger women get, the more men love football.* New York: Harcourt Brace.

Noddings, N. (1984). *Caring: A feminine approach to ethics and moral education.* New York: Ballantine Books.

Online Women: Statistics. (2007). Women in Politics. Retrieved July 18, 2007, from www.onlinewomeninpolitics.org/statistics.htm

Ott, E. M. (1989). Effects of the male-female ratio at work. Policewomen and male nurses. *Psychology of Women Quarterly, 13,* 41–57.

Padavic, I., & Earnest, W. (1994). Paternalism as a component of managerial strategy. *The Social Science Journal, 31,* 389–405.

Parker, A. (1996). The construction of masculinity within boys' physical education. *Gender and Education, 8,* 141–158.

Pascoe, C. J. (2003). Multiple masculinities? Teenage boys talk about jocks and gender. *American Behavioral Scientist, 46,* 1423–1438.

Perry, B. (2002). Childhood experience and the expression of genetic potential: What childhood neglect tells us about nature and nurture. *Brain and Mind, 3,* 79–100.

Pfister, G., Fasting, K., Scraton, S., & Vásquez, B. (1999). Women and football—A contradiction? The beginnings of women's football in four European countries. In J. A. Mangan (Ed.), *Sport in Europe: Politics, class, gender* (pp. 1–26). Portland, OR: Frank Cass.

Pilgrim, J., Martin, D., & Binder, W. (2003). Far from the finish line: Trans-sexualism and athletic competition. *Fordham Intellectual Property Media and Entertainment Law Journal, 13,* 495–550.

Popenoe, D. (1996). *Life without father: Compelling new evidence that fatherhood and marriage are indispensable for the good of children and society.* New York: Free Press.

Porteus, L. (2006, June 28). U.S. women's pro league prepares to blast back onto soccer scene. Retrieved February 23, 2007, from www.foxnews.com/story/0,2933,201438,00.html

Pringle, J. (2004). Women senior managers: Successful individuals or markers of collective change? *Women's Studies Journal, 18,* 79–98.

Pronger, B. (1990). *The arena of masculinity: Sports, homosexuality and the meaning of sex.* New York: St. Martin's Griffin.

Putney, C. (2001). *Muscular Christianity: Manhood and sports in Protestant America, 1880–1920.* Cambridge, MA: Harvard University Press.

Renold, E. (2004). "Other" boys: Negotiating nonhegemonic masculinities in the primary school. *Gender and Education, 16,* 247–266.

Reskin, B. F. (1988). Bringing the men back in: Sex differentiation and the devaluation of women's work. *Gender & Society, 2,* 58–81.

Roper, M. (1996). Seduction and succession: Circuits of homosocial desire in management. In D. L. Collinson & J. Hern (Eds), *Men as managers, managers as men: Critical perspectives on men, masculinities and managements* (pp. 210–226). London: Sage publications.

Rothman, B. K. (1983). Midwives in transition: The structure of a clinical revolution. *Social Problems, 30,* 262–271.

Rutherford, S. (2001). Any difference? An analysis of gender and divisional management styles in a large airline. *Gender, Work & Organization, 8,* 326–345.

Salt, R. E. (1991). Affectionate touch between fathers and preadolescent sons. *Journal of Marriage and the Family, 53,* 545–554.

Sandra C. (1996). Interview with Helen Sterk. *The Birthing Project Archive.* Milwaukee, WI: Marquette University Library.

Scheerder, J., Vanreusel, B., & Taks, M. (2005). Stratification patterns of active sport involvement among adults: Social change and persistence. *International Review for the Sociology of Sport, 40,* 139–162.

Schippert, C. (2003). Sporting heroic bodies in a Christian nation-at-war. Retrieved July 13, 2005, from www.usak.ca/relst/jrpc/art4–heroicbodies–print.html

Searle, J. R. (1999). *Mind, language and society: Philosophy in the real world.* New York: Basic Books.

Sears, W., & White, M. (1999). *Nighttime parenting: How to get your baby and child to sleep.* New York: Plume.

SGMA. (2004). Sports participation in America (2003 edition). Snowboarding participation report 2004. Retrieved August 29, 2005, from www.sgma.com/reports/2004/report1089722153-7142.html.

Shaw, S., & Slack, T. (2002). "It's been like that for donkey's years:" The construction of gender relations and the cultures of sport organizations. *Culture, Sport, Society, 5*, 86–106.

Sheridan, C. (2007, February 9). Amaechi becomes first NBA player to come out. Retrieved February 21, 2007, from sports.espn.go.com/nba/news/story?id=2757105

Shields, M. J., & Sparling, J. W. (1993). Father's play and touch behaviors with their three-month-old infants. *Physical & Occupational Therapy in Pediatrics, 13*(1), 39–59.

SKO. (2007). Jaarrapport 2007. [yearly report 2007] Retrieved November 15, 2008, from www.kijkonderzoek.nl/rapporten.

Solomonica-Levi, D., Yirmiya, N., Erel, O., Samet, I., & Oppenheim, D. (2001). The associations among observed maternal behavior, children's narrative representations of mothers, and children's behavior problems. *Journal of Social and Personal Relationships, 18*, 673–690.

Sommers, C. H. (2001). *The war against boys: How misguided feminism is harming our young men.* New York: Touchstone Books.

Spencer, N. (2004). Sister Act VI: Venus and Serena Williams at Indian Wells: 'Sincere fictions' and white racism. *Journal of Sport & Social Issues, 28*, 115–135.

Springen, K. (2003, January 27). Family: Bringing up baby. *Newsweek*, 72.

Stacey, J. (1996). *In the name of the father: Rethinking family values in a postmodern age.* Boston: Beacon Press.

Stackhouse, J. (2005). *Finally feminist: A pragmatic Christian understanding of gender.* Grand Rapids, MI: Baker Academic.

Statistics—women. (2007). Break the glass ceiling. Retrieved July 18, 2007, from www.breaktheglassceiling.com/statistics-women.htm

Stempel, C. (2005). Adult participation sports as cultural capital: A test of Bourdieu's theory of the field of sports. *International Review for the Sociology of Sport, 40*, 411–432.

Sterk, H. M. (2008). Gender partnership: A care theory perspective. In J. M. Curry & R. A. Wells (Eds.), *Faithful imagination in the academy.* Lanham, MD: Lexington Books.

Sterk, H. M., Hay, C., Kehoe, A., Ratcliffe, K., & Vande Vusse, L. (2002). *Who's having this baby: Perspectives on birth narratives.* Lansing: Michigan State University Press.

Stevenson, D. (2002). Women, sport, and globalization: Competing discourses of sexuality and nation. *Journal of Sport & Social Issues, 26*, 209–225.

Sugden, J. (1994). USA and the World Cup: American nativism and the rejection of the people's game. In J. Sugden & A. Tomlinson (Eds.), *Hosts and champions: Soccer cultures, national identities and the USA World Cup* (pp. 219–252). Aldershot, U.K.: Ashgate Publishing.

Swain, J. (2000). 'The money's good, the fame's good, the girls are good': The role of playground football in the construction of young boys' masculinity in a junior school. *British Journal of Sociology of Education, 21*, 95–109.

Task Force on Infant Sleep Position and Sudden Infant Death Syndrome. (2000). Changing concepts of sudden infant death syndrome: Implications for infant sleeping environment and sleep position. *Pediatrics, 105*, 650–656.

Taylor, F. W. (1911). *Principles of scientific management.* New York: Harper.

Tessier, R., Cristo, M. B., Velez, S., et al. (2003). Kangaroo mother care: A method for protecting high-risk low-birth-weight and premature infants against developmental delay. *Infant Behavior and Development, 26*, 384–397.

Thacker, S. B., & Banta, H. D. (1983). Benefits and risks of episiotomy: An interpretive review of the English language literature, 1860–1980. *Obstetrical & Gynecological Survey, 38*, 322–338.

Theberge, N. (2003). 'No fear comes': Adolescent girls, ice hockey, and the embodiment of gender. *Youth & Society, 34*, 497–516.

Tiger, L. (2000). *The decline of males: The first look at an unexpected world for men and women.* New York: Golden Books for Adults.

Townson, N. (1997). *The British at play—a social history of British sport from 1600 to the present.* Bucharest, Romania: Cavallioti Publishers.

Tronto, J. (1993). *Moral boundaries: A political argument for an ethic of care.* New York: Routledge.

Tronto, J. (2000). *Who cares? Public and private caring and the rethinking of citizenship.* Public lecture. Grand Rapids, MI: Calvin College. March 13, 2000.

UPI. (2006, December 19). Vatican soccer impossible. Retrieved February 24, 2007, from www.upi.com/NewsTrack/Quirks/20061219-121148-8375r/

U.S. Consumer Product Safety Commission. (2002, May 3). CPSC, JPMA launch campaign about the hidden hazards of placing babies in adult beds. Retrieved June 10, 2004, from www.cpsc.gov/cpscpub/prerel/prhtml02/02153.html

Van der Schaaf, M. (2005). *Identificaties in de windsurfsports. [Identity constructions of men in wind surfing].* Unpublished document. Utrecht School for Governance, University of Utrecht, Utrecht, the Netherlands.

Van der Schaaf, M. (2007*). Dare to be different: Sense making and constructions of identities by female wind surfers.* Unpublished master's thesis (in Dutch), University of Utrecht, Utrecht, the Netherlands.

Van Gemund, N., Hareman, A., Scherjon, S. A., & Kanhai, H. H. H. (2003). Intervention rates after elective induction of labor compared to labor with a spontaneous onset: A matched cohort study. *Gynecologic and Obstetric Investigation, 56*, 133–138.

Van Leeuwen, M. S., Knoppers, A., Koch, M. L., Schuurman, D., & Sterk, H. M. (1993). *After Eden: Meeting the challenge of gender reconciliation.* Grand Rapids, MI: Eerdmans.

Vatican considers forming soccer team. (2006, December 18). The Guardian Football Unlimited. Retrieved February 24, 2007, from football.guardian .co.uk/breakingnews/feedstory/0,,-6288243,00.html

Wajcman, J. (1998). *Managing like a man: Women and men in corporate management.* University Park, PA: Polity Press.

Wagner, M. (2001). Fish can't see water: The need to humanize birth. *International Journal of Gynecology & Obstetrics, 75,* 25–37.

Wagner, M. (2003). Cytotec induction and off-label use. *Midwifery Today, 67.* Retrieved January 17, 2009 from www.midwiferytoday.com/articles/cytotec.asp.

Walden, R. (2007, November 10). Jezebel can suck it (but can't breastfeed). *Women's Health News.* Retrieved March 12, 2008, from womenshealthnews .wordpress.com/2007/11/10/jezebel-can-suck-it-but-cant-breastfeed/

Warner, M. (1995). Mannen, mythen en monsters: Over vermetelheid dn bruutgeweld [Boys will be boys: The makings of the male]. *Tijdschrift voor Vrouwenstudies, 16,* 132–144.

Watson, N., Weir, S., & Friend, S. (2005). The development of muscular Christianity in Victorian Britain and beyond. *Journal of Religion & Society, 7,* 1–25.

Weber, A. M., & Meyn, L. (2002). Episiotomy use in the United States, 1979–1997. *Obstetrics & Gynecology, 100,* 1177–1182.

Weick, K. E. (1995). *Sensemaking in organizations.* Thousand Oaks, CA: Sage Publications.

Weiss, S. J., & Goebel, P. W. (2003). Parents' touch of their preterm infants and its relationship to their state of mind regarding touch. *Journal of Prenatal & Perinatal Psychology & Health, 17,* 185–202.

Weiss, S. J., Wilson, P., Hertenstein, M. J., & Campos, R. (2000, January). The tactile context of a mother's caregiving: Implications for attachment of low birth weight infants. *Infant Behavior & Development, 23,* 91–111.

Weissbluth, M. (2005). *Healthy sleep, happy child.* New York: Ballantine Books.

Wetherell, M., & Edley, N. (1999). Negotiating hegemonic masculinity: Imaginary positions and psycho-discursive practices. *Feminism & Psychology, 9,* 335–356.

Wheaton, B. (2004). *Understanding lifestyle sports: Consumption, identity and difference.* London: Routledge.

Whitehead, S. (2002). *Men and masculinities: Key themes and directions.* Cambridge, U.K.: Polity Press.

Whitehead, S., & Barrett, F. (2001). The sociology of masculinity. In S. Whitehead & F. Barrett (Eds.), *The masculinities reader* (pp. 30–35). Cambridge, UK: Polity Press.

Wilson, T. (2002). The paradox of social class and sports involvement: The roles of cultural and economic capital. *International Review for the Sociology of Sport, 37*, 5–16.

Witz, A., & Savage, M. (1992). Theoretical introduction: The gender of organizations. In M. Savage & A. Witz (Eds.), *Gender and bureaucracy* (pp. 3–60). Oxford, U.K.: Blackwell Publishers.

Wolf, N. (2001). *Misconceptions: Truth, lies, and the unexpected on the journey to motherhood.* New York: Doubleday.

Wolterstorff, N. (1983). *Until justice and peace embrace: The Kuyper lectures for 1981 delivered at the Free University of Amsterdam.* Grand Rapids, MI: Eerdman's.

Women's Statistics (n.d.) Retrieved on November 10, 2009 from www.myjax-chamber.com/upload/BreaktheGlassCeiling.pdf

Wood, J. (1993). *Who cares? Women, care and culture.* Carbondale, IL: Southern Illinois University Press.

Wood, J. (2005). *Gendered lives: Communication, gender and culture* (6th ed.). Belmont, CA: Thomson.

Woodward, A. E. (1996). Multinational masculinities and European bureaucracies. In D. L. Collinson & J. Hearn (Eds.), *Men as managers, managers as men. Critical perspectives on men, masculinities and managements* (pp. 167–187). London: Sage Publications.

Yabroff, J. (2008, January 28). Birth, the American way. *Newsweek*, 46.

Zirin, D. (2005, November 4). Sheryl Swoopes: Out of the closet—and ignored. *The Nation.* Retrieved February 14, 2007, from www.thenation.com/doc/20051121/sheryl_swoopes_out_of_the_closet

INDEX

essential understanding, of gender, xiv
ethic of care, 11, 12, 108; in birthing,
  14–15, 29; as public, 14; in sport,
  52, 66–67, 83–84; on touch, 32
ethnicity, and birthing, 27–28
ethnic minorities, as managers, 95
evangelical men's movement, 65–66
extreme sports, 61, 62–65

family: beds, 42, 44–48; demands,
  and managerial work, 89, 98;
  games, 104; touch, 48
fathers, touch of, 36, 38
Federation Internationale de Football
  Association (FIFA), 51
femininity, femininities, 5, 6–7, 58,
  61, 65; alternative, 109; conflict
  with competition, 93–94; outside
  of sport, 83
Foley catheter, 19
football, 56, 73
forceps delivery, 20
Foucault, Michel, 39

Gates, Bill, 103
gay and lesbian rights movement, 78
gay masculinities, 58
gay men, 7; in management, 96; and
  sport, 58–59
gender, 4–5; as personal choice, 9–10;
  and sexuality, 77
gender-biased language, 107
gender: biology, 4; boundaries,
  blurring of, 115–16; differences,
  Christians on, x–xi; differentiation,
  in sport, 67; equity, 10–11, 108; in
  sport, 53; identity, 4, 32; schema, 32
gendered hierarchies, 113
gendered meanings, 4–5, 107; of
  family beds, 46; of touch, 33
gendering, 108
Gerber, Ellen, 69

Gibson, Althea, 75
girls, and touch, 37–38
Goer, Henci, 23
golf, 74
good touch, 31, 48, 49
Graham, Billy, 56
Grey, John, 10
Griffin, P., 79
guilt, xiii
Gurian, Michael, 10

Hatcher, C., 97
health insurance, 16
Hearn, J., 92, 94, 104n7
heroism, 97, 112
heteronormative space, 96
heterosexism, in women's sport, 77–78
heterosexuality, 8–9, 56; and
  careerism, 101; and manliness, 54;
  and sport, 57–59, 79
hierarchical advancement, 96
higher education, women, in, 70
Hispanic women, birthing
  experience, 24–28
homebirth, 110
homophobia, 40, 77–78
homosexuality, 40; avoided by
  homosociality, 65; as vice curbed
  by sport, 53–54, 57
homosociality, 8, 65, 96, 101. See also
  male bonding
honor, 14
hospital protocols, ix, 16–19, 25, 28,
  47, 109–10
housework, 10
Hovden, J., 90
hugging, 41–42. See also touch
humanity, 2
human relations approach, to
  management, 88
human resource management
  (HRM), 88–89, 91, 94

Messcherschmidt, J., 99
Messner, A., 56, 57
metacommunication, 33, 48
Meyers, David and Holly, 35
middle management, 86, 89
midwives, 20, 21, 28, 29, 110
military, 102; metaphors, 88
Ming, Yao, 7
minority athletes, 67n3
Misoprostol, 30n2
mobility, 88, 91
modernism, 47–48
mothers, touch of, 36
motivation, 88
"muscular Christianity," 54–55, 58,
    65–66, 111
muscularity, 9, 82
mutual responsibility, 12

Naismith, James, 55
National Institute of Child Health
    and Human Development, 46
national sport, as male sport, 73
nature, realm of, 47, 71
Navratilova, Martina, 78
NBA, 76
Nelson, M. B., 56
Netherlands: birthing in, 20, 21;
    senior managers in, 91; soccer in,
    51, 61–62, 71–72, 73, 74, 79, 82
networking, 94–96
Noddings, Nel, 11
nonverbal communication, 33–34,
    49. See also touch
Norwegian sport organizations, 90

Obama, Barack, 115, 117
Olympics, 61–64, 80–81
oppressive subtexts, 114
overlapping discourses, 117

panopticon, 39

paradoxes, xi, xv, 113, 114, 118; of
    birthing, 15; of gender, 71; of
    managerial activities, 86–87, 101;
    of sporting practices, 80
parental touch, 36, 37–38, 41
parents, sleeping with children. See
    family beds
Pascoe, C. J., 61
passion, as commitment, 97
paternalism, 104n7
patriarchal dividend, 7–8, 9
peace, 114, 117
Pearson, J., 37
people skills, 112
performances, xiv–xv
physical fitness, in management,
    97–98
physicality, xii, xv, 6–7, 107;
    ungendering of, 109–13
Pitocin, 19, 25
planning, programming, budgeting
    systems (PPBS), 88
police, 102
post-feminism, ix–x, xi, 6
power, 7, 12; and gender meanings,
    33; in management, 103; and
    masculinity, 112; and sexuality,
    33, 34, 42, 49
practices, 2–4, 112–13
prejudice, 75
premature babies, 36
prenatal care, 16, 24–25
prison, 39
productivity, 88
professional relationships, adversarial
    nature of, 101
Promise Keepers, 65–66, 104n9
prostaglandins, 19, 30n2
Protestantism: feminization of, 53–54;
    and sport, 54, 66; work ethic, 104n1
puberty, 41
public relations, 94

ABOUT THE AUTHORS

Helen Sterk is professor of communication arts and sciences at Calvin College and served as department chair from 2004–2010. She held the William Spoelhof Teacher Scholar Chair at Calvin from 1997–1999. Her research interests focus on rhetoric by and about women, including analyses of popular culture, religion, and health discourses. Publications include *Gender and Applied Communication* (coedited with Patrice Buzzanell and Lynn Turner) and *Who's Having This Baby? Perspectives on Birthing*, as well as *Differences That Make a Difference* (edited with Lynn Turner) and *Constructing and Reconstructing Gender* (edited with Linda A. M. Perry and Lynn Turner). Dr. Sterk's writing has been published in journals, such as the *Western Journal of Communication* and the *Journal of Communication*, and in edited collections, such as *Evaluating Women's Health Messages: A Resourcebook*. Dr. Sterk edited the *Journal of Communication and Religion* from 2003–2006 and serves on three editorial boards. She also has served as president for the Organization for the Study of Communication, Language and Gender and the Religious Communication Association, as chapter president for the American Association of University Professors (AAUP), and as a member of the state executive board for the AAUP (Michigan).

Annelies Knoppers is a professor in the Department of Governance and Organization Studies and in the Department of Pedagogy and Educational sciences at University of Utrecht, the Netherlands. Her research interests focus on gender and ethnicity/race as they manifests themselves in the management of organizations and in the hidden curriculum in sport, health and physical education. Dr. Knoppers has served as senior editor of the Sociology of Sport Journal (2005–2009). Her research has been published in peer reviewed journals such as Sociology of Sport Journal, Journal of Sport and Social Issues; Quest; Gender, Work and Organizations; International Review for Sociology of Sport, Media, Culture and Society; Journal of Teaching Physical Education; and Sex Roles. Her last book edited with Anton Anthonissen, A. (2006) (eds.), Making Sense of Diversity in Organizing Sport (Oxford: Meyer & Meyer) was published in 2006. She serves on numerous advisory councils ranging from accreditation panels for higher education to nongovernmental organizations that aim to empower girls in developing countries through sport. She is the only and first woman to hold the position of professor in the area of sport in the Netherlands. In November 2009 she was listed as one of the 100 most influential women in the Netherlands in Opzij, a national Dutch opinion magazine.

Breinigsville, PA USA
13 December 2009
229111BV00002B/1/P